ALAN SNUGGS

SURROUNDED BY JESUS

CONFESSIONS OF A FLAWED CHRISTIAN

The right of Alan Snuggs to be identified as the
Author of the Work has been asserted by him in accordance
with the Copyright, Designs and Patents Act 1988.

Copyright © Alan Snuggs 2018

ISBN: 978-1-912535-24-8

Edited by Will Rees
Editorial: Keren Williams
Front cover by Olivia Newsome

Published by
Jelly Bean Books
Mackintosh House
136 Newport Road, Cardiff, CF24 1DJ
www.jellybeanselfpublishing.co.uk

Acknowledgements

I want to thank my wonderful wife, Nicole, who has always been my soul mate and inspiration, and my two great grown up kids, James and Jessica, who always make me smile and have the compassion of their mother.

I dedicate this book to an army of guys who were there for me in truly remarkable ways when I was at my lowest and the dark clouds hovered: Nicole, James and Jessica Snuggs; Margaret and Phil Extance; Ken and Sandy Brown; Dave and Emily Williams; Alan and Rachel Radbourne; Jo and Rich Barnforth; James and Lucianne Everall; Andy and Gill Hamill; Clive and Shannon Gerrard; Aggie Cafferky; Vicky Morten; Chris and Les Taylor; Pauline and Emyr Roberts; Wootton King; Wally and Karen Gowing; Rose Evans; Neil and Jackie Biles; Andy Woodward; Simon Bagguley; Jane and Steve Bagguley; Jon and Amanda Hewitt; Colin Baron; Tim Simmonds; Dan and Falon Terry; Alan and Samantha Newsome; Charles Newsome; Gill and Phil Everett; Keith and Alison Fletcher; Phil and Gill Berg; Barry and Karen Summers; Rachael Longley; Martin Gunther; Tim Watson and the guys at Grape and Glass; John and Karen Sadler; Tom and Caroline Gravett; Roger Swettenham; Dave Baines; Dave and Sandra Jones; Bobbie Boothroyd; Ken and Alison Foxhall; Robin Chape; Joan and Martin

Chape; Paul and Susie Quinton; Meirion Roberts; Stephen Ashurst; Andrew Astle; Richard and Karen Corran; Anthony Jeremy; Barry Mosley.

Thank you all so much. Sometimes words are never quite enough.

Alan Snuggs

Fountain of Life

All proceeds from this book will be donated to
Fountain of Life.

Fountain of Life is a UK registered Christian charity that is dedicated to improving the lives of some of the poorest people in India, including tribal people, who are so often neglected, looked down upon and ignored.

We are committed to giving them dignity and value, equipping them with essential skills, and caring for the ones who have no one else to look after them. We run tailoring centres and literacy schools in their villages, and we now have built and run a home for abandoned children, which provides a loving, nurturing environment for these children, some of whom have various forms of disabilities. We aim to look after them to a high standard, helping each one to feel like an individual and a cherished part of a loving family, supporting them to reach their potential.

It is so rewarding to see them grow, change and thrive. We distribute aid and offer support where needed amongst sixty-four villages, positively impacting communities for good, and as we build these bridges we are able to share with them the love and hope that comes from knowing Jesus.

Sundar and Sarah Pinninty

www.flmhope.org   flmhopeindia@gmail.com

For you are the Fountain of Life, the light by which we see.
Psalm 36:9

Contents

Preface

This is how I fight my battles.
It may look like I'm surrounded,
but I'm surrounded by you.
Michael W Smith

I wanted to write a book about God that was brutally honest. I am told that too many Christian books focus on triumph and success. Like most people, my life has been mixed. There were years when everything, whether career or church stuff, turned to pure gold. But then there were also other darker moments, moments when I thought the storms of life were going to overwhelm me, moments when I thought the sun had left the sky, moments that I'd prefer to forget: failures, bad decisions, sin, struggles and a short but terrible period of depression and illness.

God is constant. He is always there, in the sunshine as well as the rain. And this book, which contains twenty-four chapters on different themes, is about celebrating what we have in Jesus, whatever the circumstances. I hope it encourages and inspires you to trust him even more that I'm sure you already do. I also hope it will make you smile.

This book is about Jesus, not me. He is the big story. He is the highway. God has put us on a stage. It's his dance floor, and we are meant to dance with him. We can all have a sense of destiny and be part of God's great story. The title of this book reflects what I know to be true. In every battle, in every moment of our lives we are surrounded by Jesus, even when we can't see it or feel it. The king is for us. We may all be flawed, but he has all the answers.

It was always meant to be this way.

Alan Snuggs, September 2018

Chapter One
Where It All Started:
London, God Shouts Out

*So how can you say that you're lonely, and say for you
that the sun don't shine?
Let me take you by the hand and lead you through the
streets of London.
I'll show you something to make you change your
mind...*
Ralph McTell, 'The Streets of London'

In September 1981, I joined the Metropolitan Police on
their graduate scheme. The initial training at Hendon,
London, was to be the toughest thing I would ever do. It
was relentless. Rote learning, physical exercise, riot
training, lectures... I worked twelve hours a day, and each
week someone was asked to leave my class. You never
knew if it was going to be you!

I had massive ambition: maybe to be the next police
commissioner, perhaps to get to commander, to earn
money, certainly to marry a beautiful woman. But the
one ambition I definitely didn't have at that time was to
become a Christian.

I passed the police training, much to my relief, and

then began a two year probation based in Chiswick and Brentford, West London, which included some of the toughest estates in the capital. I was confident, in retrospect maybe a little arrogant, but I was in for a big culture shock.

On my first day, I casually walked down the street from the police station and said good morning to an elderly couple. The man spat at me and muttered 'kid copper' – and that was just the start! The next day I was sent to sort out a married couple in their fifties; this wasn't just your average domestic – they were trying to kill each other! And so it went on: drugs, alcohol, fights, riots, traffic accidents, car chases, court appearances, even suspected bombs... I saw death several times, including witnessing the tragic death of a young police officer during training, and a fourteen-year-old lad hanging from a tree.

Probably my worst experience was to stand with two elderly parents as they viewed the body of their only son, just thirty years old, who had been killed in a motor cycle accident. I will never forget their grief, or the fact that they thanked me for helping them when all I could do was to stand with them and sympathise. I grew up fast – my very survival depended on it.

I soon began to toughen up, and found with experience that I was good at calming even the most hostile situations. I passed my probation and was given the task of investigating burglaries; I made some quality arrests and soon became part of a riot squad, which I loved, as to keep fit we played football four hours a day!

In my five years as a copper, I saw a lot of life, and looking back I was privileged to do so. I met stars like

Richard Briars, the Three Degrees and Des Lyman. I also met murderers and the poorest in society. I saluted Ronald Regan, and once, for a dare, broke into the American Embassy bar with my squad, only to be apprehended by the American military. But much of the work was routine, mundane and hard.

In many ways in those days I had it all. I had met my beautiful wife, Nicole, who had come to London at eighteen to escape her home life. We knew right from the start we would always be together. I had a good job. I lived in a flat slap bang next to Buckingham Palace, and I owned a new car. But inside I was struggling. I knew something was missing.

I had been encouraged to go to a church near to where I lived. My flat was managed by the church, so I felt obliged to put in an appearance. The church was St Michael's, Chester Square, and it was *posh*. However, the people seemed friendly, challenging my stereotypes. Not to mention the young people met in a pub after the service, which certainly met with my approval!

One day a guy called David Watson, a renowned clergyman and prolific Christian author*, came to the church and talked about Jesus. I went with Nicole, interested to see what was said; after all I was a Christian, wasn't I? I knew who God was, anyway.

But David talked about a totally different God to the one I thought I knew. He said that God loved me so much he had sent his son, Jesus, to blot out all my sin and give me a new life, not just in eternity but here right now. I had never heard this. He asked anyone who wanted to get to know Jesus to stand up. Now, no way was I going to stand up; I was far too cool. But I suddenly found myself on my feet. I looked round and so was Nicole. I felt a deep peace inside that I had never felt before. I had become a Christian – truly a Christian: a believer.

My life did not change overnight. I remained fairly arrogant, and the church found me difficult in those early days. I joined a small group of Christians in what was called a home group. Part of that group was a lovely woman called Eleanor Mumford; later, she and her husband John were to form the Vineyard Church in the UK, which is still growing today. (And if you were thinking there might be a connection with the group Mumford and Sons, you'd be right: Eleanor and John are the parents of the lead singer, Marcus.) Back then, Eleanor always used to ask me for a lift to group. I realise now that she never needed a lift; she just wanted to talk to me about Jesus. I then met a guy called John Wimber, who started a spiritual revival in this country. He taught us about something called the Holy Spirit. I didn't even know that God had a Holy Spirit!

With people like that around me, I started to get it more and more. Nicole and I began to see miracles and people's lives being changed forever. We didn't realise at the time that people like John Wimber and the Mumfords were going to be seen as groundbreakers. We just went with the flow.

I knew that my life was changing when fellow police officers started to say things like, 'So are you one of those nice care bear Christians?' But I also met police officers who were, in their own words, 'born again Christians', including a larger than life sergeant who once dragged me into a cell to reassure me that I was not on my own. I still found the job challenging at times, but I started to hear God speaking to me. One day, walking down a side street in Chiswick, I told him I was lonely. The answer came back: 'I know, but you are never alone.'

David Watson joined our church in London, and I was thrilled. But within months we were given devastating news. David had inoperable cancer. I was angry and confused. Why had God allowed this? David got worse and worse, his cancer becoming the subject of national focus as thousands of people prayed for his healing. Sadly, it was not to be, but his last public talks were to have an impact on my life that has defined me ever since.

Nicole and I were asked to attend David's final two sermons. This was a man who had spoken in front of thousands, but we were privileged to be in an audience of just thirty to hear his last words. His remarkable final talk was around Psalm Ninety One.

'Whoever dwells in the shelter of the most high will rest in the shadow of the almighty, I will say of the Lord, he is my refuge and my fortress, and my God in whom I trust.'

There wasn't a dry eye in the house.

David sat on a stool, in obvious pain and discomfort, but with eyes that shone and a smile that lit up the room. He said this about Jesus: 'I know it's true, I know he is with me, I know where I am going, the best is yet to be.'

Now you can believe a man like that!

David died and I was deeply saddened. But I knew that, despite my failings, my life was never going to be the same. I was a one hundred percent, down the line, full on, in your face Jesus follower. I was signed up hook, line and sinker.

I was never going back.

* David's story is contained in the remarkable book *Fear No Evil*.

Chapter Two
Locked In a Cell

I was not born with a hunger to be free. I was born free, free in every way that I could know.
Nelson Mandela

I was once asked to introduce myself to a group of church leaders. The challenge was to 'Tell us something unusual about yourself'. I had to think on the spot, which, as anyone who knows me well could tell you, always causes a little concern! I responded, 'I think I could fairly safely say that I am the only person in this room who has been arrested and thrown in a cell.' Well, that caused a stir, I can tell you. The awkwardness of the subsequent silence was palpable. I waited for a further moment and then explained.

As you know, I was a policeman in Chiswick, London, during the early nineteen eighties. However, I never really looked like a policeman. For a start, I was only five foot seven and three quarters. The force's full entry requirements specified that officers had to be at least five foot eight, but because I was already on the graduate course by the time they realised their mistake, they decided to let me in anyway. Embarrassingly, I also looked about fourteen years old. You might think I'm exaggerating, but I was once harangued by an elderly woman for being a 'baby copper' and 'a disgrace to my nation'! Still, there was one advantage: because I didn't look like a police officer, my colleagues often decided I was suited to work undercover.

In those days I worked regularly with a police officer called Bill Surtees. Bill was near retirement and was reputed to be the best driver in the Met. He was also six feet four – he towered over a little chap like me! When he was first told he would be working with me, he let out a few choice expletives that my sheltered upbringing had not quite prepared me for. However, over the next few weeks, he realised that, despite my physical shortcomings, I could do one thing better than him: I could run! As long as he drove me to the right place at the right time, few bad guys would ever escape me.

Over time, we became a pretty good team, him driving us at ridiculous speeds towards any potential arrests, and me able to keep up with anyone who decided to make a run for it. On one occasion we chased a car down the M4 at over one hundred and twenty miles an hour, a police helicopter overhead. That was ace! And together, we once made a very famous arrest – but that is another story!

We became firm friends with Bill and his wife, Sue, who even came to our wedding. I loved working with Bill. He was supremely professional, had impeccable standards and was a guy you never messed with. But he was also one of the kindest and most decent men I have ever met. Not to mention, the biggest wind up merchant.

On one particular spring day, we were in charge of

the district crime car. Bill dropped me off in Richmond, West London. There was a gang of car thieves operating in this area, and I was detailed to follow them and at the right moment call in the rest of my team. Unfortunately, communications were especially poor in those days, and the Richmond crew apparently had no idea I was there. I came across a gang of eight youths in the act of stealing an old Ford Capri, but before I could call my guys, the Richmond police swooped in and arrested the gang. A good day's work, you might say. However, they also arrested me! Despite my protests, they locked me in a van with two of the gang. 'Who the flip are you?' one of them asked. Now think about it – what would you have said? I muttered something about criminal damage and then enjoyed my ride back to Richmond police station, where I thought all would be sorted out. But it wasn't. I was booked into the custody suite by a grim-faced sergeant then led to a cell. As I entered the door, I saw Bill from the corner of my eye.

'Tell them who I am, Bill, for goodness' sake!' I shouted.

A reply came back which I have never ever forgotten: 'I have never seen this man before in my life.' At which point the cell doors banged shut.

Now, I knew it was all a wind up, but it was an odd feeling being shut in that cell, especially as I can get a bit claustrophobic. I hate lifts and small spaces with a passion. Bill got his full money's worth, leaving me in that dark place for over an hour before he came to let me out. I shouted a few choice words at him, and made him promise to buy me tea for the next month as compensation, but I could see the funny side of it.

But here's the thing. Apparently whilst I was sat in that cell, the door was never locked. I could have walked out at any time. That is what reminds me of the gospel. Many of us think that we are too bad, too far away from God for him to possibly want to come and save us. We sit in our own self-made cell thinking we are stuffed, closed in, imprisoned by our sin and muck. But Jesus has freed us already. He did it on the cross. He has opened the door; we just have to walk out. The apostle Paul, who knew a thing about imprisonment, puts it like this: 'It is for freedom that Christ has set us free, stand firm then and do not let yourselves be burdened by a yoke of slavery.'

Walking out of a cell is easy if someone has taken the trouble to open the door for you.

I last saw Bill Surtees a month before I left the Met back in 1985. I was driving along Chiswick High Road, having finished an early shift, when a Rover 3.5 police car came alongside me, deliberately shunting me into a bus lane and forcing me to come to a shuddering halt behind a stationary bus.

I didn't even have to look. I knew it was Bill.

Chapter Three
Different Kicks

Injustice anywhere is a threat to justice everywhere.
Martin Luther King Jr

I often look back on my five years in the Metropolitan police with wonder. It certainly wasn't dull. As a riot policeman and general bobby, I got to see a lot of things, including some life-changing historical events. For example, I was there when WPC Yvonne Fletcher was shot by a coward firing from the Libyan Embassy. I also managed to get lost and isolated from my team in the second Brixton riot, only to be saved by a BBC Panorama crew that had also lost its way in the maze of Brixton's streets. And there were also some bizarre experiences, like smashing down a door and terrifying a couple who were making love; we'd thought that their various noises were suspects on the premises!

But two things stand out as particularly memorable: two different kicks in two quite different places.

The tale of the first kick is relatively amusing – in hindsight, anyway! One day I was informed that, as a probationer, I was to be attached to the regional bomb car. Now, that sounded exciting, not to mention quite technical. It wasn't! A rather grumpy, seasoned PC turned up in an old red Avenger. As a raw recruit, having no idea what an explosive device even looked like, I naively asked what I was supposed to do. He gave me a kind of 'you silly boy' look, and proceeded to drive us aimlessly around central London.

For hours nothing happened, but just as I was beginning to think that it might all just be one big wind up, out of the blue we got a call. There was apparently a suspect package near Harrods; wires had been spotted protruding from a street refuse bin. I was immediately unnerved. What on earth was I supposed to do? Surely trained bomb disposal people would be called?

But no. My silent friend parked up a few hundred yards away from the package. By this time a small crowd had gathered. They were being held back by a local constable. Then I heard some words I will never forget: 'Just go and give it a kick.'

Yes, this actually happened! I was instructed to kick the suspect package to see if it went off! Now, I was a probationer, and I had been taught to do everything as I was instructed. At Hendon Training School, as part of our 'education', we had once been told to run outside in our clean white gym kit and lie in a muddy puddle – just for the hell of it! We followed every command to the absolute letter. So I did what was told. Inwardly I said my farewells, and then I kicked the bin.

Fortunately, it all turned out to be a false alarm. The 'bomb' was just a radio that someone had thrown away. I returned to my helpful colleague, who simply nodded and started to fill in a detailed report. I was shaking and white as a sheet. 'Well done,' he muttered, 'nice job.'

Then I realised: this happened every day! This buffoon picked up some unsuspecting probationer and used them as cannon fodder. He never got out of the car. In his eyes, we were obviously exceedingly expendable.

This story does, though, have a bitter twist. Some months later a bomb really did go off outside Harrods, killing two police officers. In fact, my friend Mark almost lost his life: he took that call, only to be stood down after the officers who were killed told him that they were nearer to the scene.

The other kick that stands out comes from my experience of the miners' strike. I spent three weeks in Nottinghamshire, along with my riot squad, supposedly protecting the Nottinghamshire miners from the Yorkshire lads who had come down to stop them from breaking the strike. We did twenty hour shifts every day, and I even got to go down into a coal mine to see the incredibly brave work that these guys did. I remember seeing a sign that read 'I am glad I am British, I am glad I am free, but I wish I were a dog and Scargill were a tree'. An interesting statement given that Scarghill would eventually prove to be right: all the mines in Britain would close.

There were scuffles, and on one occasion the bricks came flying, but all in all there was more banter than violence. I had recently married Nicole, who was from Yorkshire, so I used this to break the ice with the Yorkshire miners. On the whole I found them to be decent men with great humour who were just standing up for what they believed.

One day I saw a police officer from another unit in the Met approach one of the guys I had been talking to.

He kicked him hard on the shins. The Yorkshire miner unsurprisingly hit him back and a fight ensued. The poor guy was dragged off to a van and I imagine subsequently charged with assault. The Met officer had done this for one reason: money. He would have to come back to Nottinghamshire and give evidence in court. That would give him plenty of overtime. I felt incensed and sick at the same time. But there was nothing I could do. It happened in a flash amidst many exchanges and confrontations. Sometimes I wondered which side I was on.

A little later, I went to a Yorkshire pub with Nicole to meet her dad. As I walked in, the pub went silent. The word was out that I was a London copper and I had been posted up North during the miners' strike. I was not welcome. I walked to the bar wondering if I would get out unscathed. Nicole's dad walked over and put a pint in front of me. 'Sup up, lad,' he said in his thick Yorkshire accent, loudly enough for everyone to hear. At that point people started talking again, leaving me be. Her dad had saved me from a kicking. Sometimes scars run deeper than we will ever know.

Looking back, I think the miners were very harshly treated. Yes, a small minority were excessive in their actions and probably deserved to be dealt with by the courts. But despite the odds being heavily stacked against them, the vast majority were simply trying to protect their way of life, their livelihoods, their communities and their children's future. They deserved much more than they got. Some of those communities are still ghost towns today. There were no winners, only losers.

When you read the Bible, particularly the Psalms and

prophets like Jeremiah, they describe a God who is passionate about justice. The Bible doesn't pretend that bad things don't happen. What it does, though, is explain that beyond terrible evils there is always the hope of real justice. His justice. God is outraged at injustice and unfairness, and one day everything will be exposed, even sly kicks on the shin. Justice will flow like a river. One day Jesus will bring true justice to this grubby world.

I for one will give a loud shout for the Yorkshire miners.

Chapter Four
Gordon Ramsey Has a Point

I want what you got.
Kostya Agrivovich, St Petersburg, 1994

'There has got to be more than this!'
These are words I have heard from so many, even those who you would have thought had everything. The rich, the famous, the successful -- even they often yearn for more ordinary things: a happy family, a great partner or a successful business.

I was struck by the words of the colourful TV chef Gordon Ramsey, who reflected on his life in his autobiography:

'When I think about myself, I still see a little boy who is desperate to escape and desperate to please. The fact that I've long since escaped, and long since been pleasing people, has had little or no impact. I just keep going, moving as far away from where I began as possible.'

Is life futile? King Solomon is one of the greatest kings in the Old Testament, and said to be the wisest. He did amazing things, changing his country beyond recognition. During his reign, almost all of the Promised Land lay in his hands, and Israel was at peace. It is said that Solomon made silver as common as stones. Yet his fall eventually brought the kingdom crashing down.

Solomon asks in Ecclesiastes: 'What is it all for? Meaningless, meaningless! Utterly meaningless! Everything is meaningless. What does man gain from all his labour, at which he toils under the sun?'

What is clear from all our experience is that no amount of self pleasure, achievement or success is going to give us real lasting peace – accepting, of course, that there is momentary joy to be found in many things.

I remember talking to a businessman called Dave. Dave was rich and successful and planning an early retirement involving several holidays a year, and still more moneymaking on the stock market.

'But what happens after that?' I said.

'Well, you've got me there,' Dave replied. 'But that's such a long time away. I don't need to worry about that right now. I don't need your God.'

At one stage during our conversation, he threw up a V sign. 'That's what I think of your God,' he said.

Dave sadly died two weeks later, from a heart attack that no one, certainly not he, had seen coming. His words, and that violent gesture, have stayed with me ever since.

Could it be that God has the answer and it is staring us all right in the face? Is there someone he might have sent who makes everything meaningful? The Old Testament is full of amazingly accurate prophecies, made thousands of years before Jesus was born, prophecies that no atheist has ever been able to explain. They are predictions about Jesus: how he would be born, how he would live, how he would die. They are unerringly accurate, predicting key details like the fact he would ride into Jerusalem on a donkey, and that Roman soldiers would draw lots for his clothes.

The Old Testament promised someone who would give us hope, someone who would come down to this rotten little earth and save us from ourselves. He would answer a key question: 'Who is it that can overcome death?' The answer given is Jesus. In my early life I never really got this. Just looking at the wonder of the stars, I knew there must be a God above me, but I never thought he would be interested in me.

Many years ago, in Saint Petersburg, Russia, I spoke to a young man called Kostya about Jesus. I was part of a group of young people from the UK who wanted to share their faith. For a number of days, I shared my story, but each time he turned sadly away – it was not for him.

On the last night we were there, I looked for Kostya, but our meeting had long started and there was no sign of him. My heart sank. But then I heard someone running down the corridor to our meeting room. In rushed Kostya.

'I want what you got!' he shouted, and there and then gave his life to Jesus.

Could it be that this is the answer for the whole world, even Gordon Ramsey, even you and me? Jesus is the one that can give you the significance your human soul is yearning for. Kostya found it that night.

The world needs Jesus.

He's got what you want.

Chapter Five
Even Multiple Murderers Love Their Gran

Although my memory is fading, I remember two things very clearly: I am a great sinner and Christ is a great saviour.
John Newton

So there I was, enjoying a pint with my mate Steve, when suddenly he brought up the subject of Christianity.

'Let me just say this,' he said, pointedly, 'I consider myself a good person. I don't go to church, I don't believe in Jesus, but I am a decent sort of bloke. I give money to charity and treat everyone around me in a good way. Surely I will go to heaven.'

I wasn't sure if it was a statement or a question, but I took it as the latter.

'The thing is, mate, you certainly are a good bloke, and I often find the most decent, kindest people are non-Christians, but no one is good enough to reach God's standards.'

Steve looked a little offended. 'Well, I don't know how it works then. Surely Christianity is all about keeping rules and being a good person, and I think I do all of that.'

I explained that he had got Christianity wrong, that Christianity is all about knowing Jesus, about faith and belief in him. I decided to illustrate my point through a little exercise.

'On a scale of one to ten, where do you rate God in terms of being perfect and good?'

'Well, I guess a ten,' said Steve.

'OK,' I said, 'on a scale of one to ten where would you rate Adolf Hitler?'

'That's easy,' he replied. 'I'd give him half a point.' He explained that the half was because Hitler liked dogs, which was a little lost on me, but there you go.

'What about Mother Theresa?'

'I think nine, because, although she was marvellous, she was still human, so she couldn't have been perfect.'

I smiled; Steve was beginning to get the point.

'So where would you rate me?' I asked.

He looked sheepish. 'Well, Alan, you are a good sort of guy, even though you're a West Ham supporter so maybe an eight.'

I was suitably relieved! 'And where do you fit on the scale?'

'Probably a six.'

This was typical of his humble nature, I thought.

'Now,' I said, 'what links Hitler, Mother Theresa, you and me?'

He hesitated for a few seconds, and then out came a pearl of wisdom.

'I guess we are all falling short of God's standards!' he replied.

Steve was spot on. The Bible tells us clearly that no

one is good apart from God, and that our sin is something that God needed to deal with in a just and righteous way. He did that by sending Jesus, who sorted our sin on the cross forever.

As Paul in his letter to the Romans reminds us: 'There is no one righteous, not even one, for all have sinned and fall short of the glory of God.'

Paul tells us that, through his sacrifice, Jesus justifies all of us who believe, that through Jesus none of us who believe in him will be condemned. Of course, Paul knew all about sin. Before he found Jesus, he ruthlessly killed and imprisoned many Christians.

Let me go back to Steve's observation that I was a 'good sort of guy'. It was flattering to be told such, but like everyone else I am capable of bad things, bad thoughts and sin. Indeed, there are things that I have done that make me feel utterly ashamed.

Appearances can be deceptive. Many years ago, when I was a police officer, I was asked to sit with a prisoner for two hours. He was being questioned for over forty eight hours by the CID. His name was Mike, and he seemed like a really nice guy. I didn't ask him what he had done; instead we chatted about football, his family, the weather and so on. He told me that he phoned his gran every day. He waved me a cheery good bye as the CID officers reappeared.

I asked the duty sergeant what he was in for. 'Oh, him, he's a multiple killer. A real psycho, a really dangerous man. Gives me the creeps!'

I shuddered. I had been happily chatting away with a murderer (though we should, of course, judge no one)! Even multiple murderers phone their gran!

But equally, because God made us in his image, we are all capable of great acts of kindness, generosity and love. But appearances are deceptive. The reality is that we are all sinners. We all fall short of God's standards. In Genesis, we are told that when man fell away, sin and death entered the world. You can see this even in the most innocent child. Just watch how sin can take hold, how even in a healthy, positive, loving environment children will, intentionally, disobey their parents. We remain just the same: capable of great good, but all essentially flawed.

I, for one, am grateful that we have a loving father who didn't condemn us, who sent his one and only son to bring us all home: Steve, Mother Theresa, me, you and even those that we wouldn't consider eligible.

Heaven is full of blessed and loved believers who screwed up. The only good guy is God.

Now that *is* good news!

Chapter Six
The Real Messi

A man who was merely a man and said the sort of things Jesus said would not be a great moral teacher. He would either be a lunatic... or else he would be the Devil of Hell. You must make your choice. Either this man was, and is, the Son of God: or else a madman or something worse. You can shut Him up for a fool, you can spit at Him and kill Him as a demon; or you can fall at His feet and call Him Lord and God. But let us not come with any patronising nonsense about His being a great human teacher. He has not left that open to us. He did not intend to.
CS Lewis

My friend Jane phoned me yesterday. Jane is bipolar and has more problems than most anyone I know, but she has a wonderful knack of cutting right to the chase.

'Alan,' she said, 'my brother has cancer, and I am trying to share my faith with him, but he is convinced that all religions are the same. Can you pray for him?'

Well, I did, but I also got to thinking about that very thorny question: are all religions the same? What right do we have to say that Christianity is the only way to God? And as it was the night of the Champion League semi-finals, I also began to think about Lionel Andres Messi.

Messi is a superstar. He is five foot seven of Argentinian footballing genius. Messi can do things with a football that the rest of his peers could only dream of. Many view him as the greatest footballer that has ever played, and he had scored again for his club team, Barcelona, that weekend.

Some years ago, Nicole and I went to Barcelona for a romantic weekend. We booked a bus pass that would take us to all the famous places in Barcelona, including the Nou Camp – Barcelona's prestigious football stadium – where Messi plays and trains. (Not that this site was particularly high on Nicole's agenda!)

As we approached the stadium on the tour bus, I noticed a huge crowd gathering just outside the front gates. Standing in the middle of the crowd was a young, athletic-looking man in a smart black suit. He was holding a large gold trophy. Someone on the bus shouted, 'Messi, Messi!'

I was so excited. I was going to see the great man himself. Messi had obviously come out from his training session to greet his fans. What an opportunity! I jumped up, camera in hand.

However, something made me sit back down again. People were not only taking photographs of Messi, but also, bizarrely, handing him money. Then I noticed a local policeman approach, at which point the young man shoved his trophy in a bag and ran for it. It was a con. This wasn't Messi. This was a lookalike pretending to be

Messi, and even the people who gave him money knew he wasn't the real deal.

Jesus claimed to be the only way and the only truth. Indeed, he made claims that no one else has ever made. Here are some of them:

- That he was also God
- That he was the son of God
- That he came from heaven
- That he performed miracles
- That our sins needed to be dealt with and only he could save us
- That he came to die on a cross for our sins
- That we could only get access to God through him
- That he is coming back one day to create a new heaven and a new earth

Many people throughout history have claimed to speak for God. Very few have ever claimed to be God. Even great religious figures such as Buddha, Krishna and Muhammad didn't claim to be God. In fact, most of them explicitly encouraged their followers *not* to think of them as God.

Although I fully respect all world religions, and accept they have much from which we can learn, their founders lie dead in the grave. They don't have an answer to the one thing that concerns us all: our own mortality.

Christians believe that Jesus overcame death and dealt with our sin. He is the real deal, the only king in town. Everyone has a choice but I, like billions of others, have come to believe that the God who made this world also sent Jesus, his one and only son, to save us from ourselves. I for one am profoundly grateful.

So, here is a question, and it's a really important one: do you want the real thing?

Chapter Seven
Inclusive Jesus

We are commanded to humble ourselves: nowhere are we commanded to humble others.
PJ Smyth

'I feel invisible. I'm bottom of the pile, and I may as well not exist.'

I have heard that particular statement so many times. In fact, I have said similar things myself.

I recently heard it from a friend who works in a school. Staff there ignore her, walking by without a word. I have heard it from a guy on a factory production line, where the floor manager doesn't know his name. I have heard it in the workplace, in social clubs, on streets, in families. And I hear it from people in churches, which is more of a worry to me than anything else.

In my early days in the Met, I remember being told by an officer who was 'puppy walking' me that I would not be accepted until I had proven myself. I shouldn't expect to be invited in for a cuppa for several weeks. At a time when I needed encouragement and support, he made me feel like a piece of dirt. I soon realised that it was only he who was excluding me, and that he gave this pathetic speech to every recruit.

Two years later, now a 'puppy walker' myself, I resolved to always welcome and support new officers. I knew what it was like to be excluded.

Most of us will have been *that* person. The one who is excluded. The one who isn't part of the party. The couple who are not invited to the wedding, the people who don't get asked for a drink down the pub. Of course, there are varying degrees and extremes, different kinds of exclusion: maybe it's being left out in a work or a social setting, or maybe it is exclusion due to colour, ethnicity, sexuality, financial standing, religion, disability, age. You name it, it exists.

My own life experience is that even when you think you are being totally inclusive, others may not see it that way. And they are probably right!

I want to remind you of the most inclusive person of all: Jesus.

Jesus reached out to those who were alienated in society. Lepers; prostitutes; tax collectors; Pharisees; Romans; Samaritans; adulterers and, yes, women! He had a compassion and love that was simply stunning.

He would eat and drink with sinners, getting up the noses of the righteous leaders of the day. But as he said himself, there will be more rejoicing in heaven over one sinner who repents than over ninety-nine righteous persons who do not need to repent.

This was the kind of heresy that would get him crucified.

One of my favourite stories is the story of Zacchaeus, a chief tax collector. He was not the sort of guy you would have asked to a party. At the sight of him, most people of his day would have crossed to the other side of the road. He would have been hated by the Jews for collaborating with the Romans, making himself rich at the Jews' expense. His testimony would not have been accepted in a Jewish court. His offering was not acceptable in the Temple. He was marginalised and excluded. He was labelled as scum.

Luke tells us that, as Jesus entered Jericho, Zacchaeus went to see him. But being a short man, he could not see past the large crowd that had assembled. So he ran ahead and climbed a sycamore tree. When Jesus reached that spot, he looked up and said, 'Zacchaeus, come down immediately. I must stay at your house today.' So Zacchaeus came down and welcomed Jesus gladly, and for good measure decided to give half of his possessions to the poor.

The people around Jesus muttered, saying, 'He has gone to be the guest of a sinner.'

But Jesus said to them, 'Today salvation has come to this house because this man too is a son of Abraham. For the son of man came to seek and to save what was lost.'

What a party there must have been that night! Imagine who was there: Simon Peter, a humble fisherman, bold as brass; Simon the Zealot – it's unlikely he was dull! Lazarus raised from the dead; Mary the ex prostitute; Simon the leper, who was, no longer a leper... All kinds of interesting and exotic characters, and Jesus loved them all.

The truth is that Jesus loves you. The Bible tells us that he even knows how many hairs you have on your head. You are not invisible. To him you are precious. To him you are someone worth saving. The king is on your side. To him you belong.

He has always been looking for you.

As I write, I am thinking of my church home group. We are a bunch of people that get together every week to talk about life. It's an interesting mix.

There's Bob, on the surface a hugely successful business man, confident in every way, but with a history of terrible depression. Then there's Liz, the life and soul of every party, yet nursing a deep sadness over the tragic loss of her three year old daughter many years ago. There's Sean, a great family man who, having been made redundant several times, worries that he may not be able to provide for his family. Chris, a recovering alcoholic. Julie, a brilliant worship leader but struggling with doubts about the Christian faith. Rick, like a father figure to us all, but still grieving over the fact that his own father left him at the age of twelve.

And then there's me. I know all these people and they know me. My doubts, my flaws, my awkwardness, my idiosyncrasies. That's how we do life together. Total honesty, total acceptance. We also try to treat those around us in the same way. We might fail to be always inclusive, like Jesus, but we go on trying because he told us to do it and he knows what we all need.

If we want folk to get to know our Jesus then we need to be Jesus to everyone around us. We won't be remembered for our successes, our opinions or our financial standing.

We will be remembered for our love

Chapter Eight
Over the Top Tacklers

There are a lot of people around who can't wait to tell you what you've done wrong, but there aren't many fathers willing to take the time and effort to help you grow up.
One Corinthians, Four (The Message Bible)

Men view church-going like a prostate exam. It's something that can save their lives but it's so unpleasant and invasive they put it off.
David Murrow

Whatever church environment I have worked in, one thing has never changed. If any guy is seen as a bit of a challenge, they will end up at my door. My wife would say it's because I know how to talk to them. Truth is, I feel a bit like them. I have some jagged edges myself. But one thing I know is that Jesus loves the rough diamonds too.

This morning I had breakfast with three guys. All of them have a past. All of them follow Jesus. One of them, Colin, was an atheist for years. He was also an alcoholic. Colin told us that every day for twenty years he drank a bottle of vodka. We were all amazed he made it through. He also admitted to having been a bit of a bruiser, someone who would strike out first and ask questions later.

Yet the transformation in his life has been nothing short of a miracle. He is still the same cheeky Colin, but now he radiates Jesus. He has a gentleness about him that has amazed his friends and those he works with. He recently got married, he's fitter and more active than he has ever been, and his business is thriving.

And here's the thing: I have seen this so many times before. Guys restored, forgiven, changed forever and walking with the saviour. It's not an earthly miracle – it's Jesus.

When I met him, many years ago, it was said of Angus that if you wanted someone beaten up, he was the man to sort it! He was once offered a criminal job in my presence. He hurriedly explained that I was the local pastor, and he didn't do that kind of stuff anymore. Angus has had a really tough past. His father beat him up most days. Once he even gave him some pills and told him to go commit suicide.

We became friends, and one of the first things I was able to help him with was the pain of losing his mother to cancer. He asked me to speak at the funeral. Little did I know that, to save money, he had organised for me to conduct the whole ceremony! I only found out as I entered the crematorium, when the funeral director asked me when I would want to press the button for the body to 'go down'. Apparently I went as white as a sheet!

And that's Angus: always trying his luck. He stunned the whole town of Buxton – not to mention himself –

when he became a Christian. But he loves God and isn't afraid to tell everyone and anyone. I used to think that if Angus asked you to become a Christian, you would probably do it for fear of your life! Angus is still a little unconventional. For example, it took me some years to convince him that stealing a key ring from Harrods for a dare wasn't really what God wanted for his life. But there is no one I know that loves Jesus more than Angus.

John was a tough Brummy. We met several years ago when his wife started coming to our church. He most definitely wasn't going to join us on a Sunday, but he did like playing football. I happened to be the church football manager, and we agreed that I would put John straight into our team on condition that I could tell him about Jesus. After several challenging evenings together, God 'got him' and he became a Christian. Many years later, I was privileged to watch John giving the address at the funeral of his father-in-law. He was a different man, oozing grace and love. He spoke magnificently, with an authority and a sureness that could only have come from God. It made me cry, I was that proud.

The apostle Paul understood the rough diamonds too. He says in his letter to the Corinthians that guys have many guardians, but not many fathers. Here he is reminding us that guys have many around them who will criticise and try to regulate their behaviour, but few who will guide them, walk with them and help them through life. It seems to me that we all need a father.

Back to my friend Brummy John. The truth is that, despite his becoming a Christian, there was little kindness and grace about his tackling as our new central midfielder. In his first game it took him just five minutes to be sent off, for a challenge that would have made Vinnie Jones wince.

As John stomped off, giving the referee the finger, one of my team mates muttered, 'What the heck was that?'

'That, my friend, is a work in progress,' I replied, 'and beautiful it is too.'

Chapter Nine
A Ferocious Dad

But while he was still a long way off, his father saw
him and was filled with compassion for him. He ran to
his son, threw his arms around him and kissed him.
Jesus Christ, from the story of the prodigal son

In my younger days I thought of God as austere, even
ferocious. This was born of the kind of religion I
experienced as a child. Like much of my generation, as
a child I went to church but never quite understood why.

My father was a good, caring, hard working man, and
he did his best to be a good dad. But when I was young,
he had little time for me. In fact, I cannot recall any time
that we spent as just father and son. I longed for him to
take me to see AFC Bournemouth, our local football
team. My friends all went with their dads. But it was not
to be. Throughout my early years, I viewed him as an
authoritarian figure, who would slipper me when I was
bad and for the rest of the time ignore me.

I was a good rugby player and was always hugely
disappointed that my father never found the time to come
and watch me. Only once, under acute pressure from my
mum, did he turn up on the sidelines. I scored two tries

that match, only to find out afterwards that in the thick fog he couldn't see who had scored! This kind of summed up our relationship.

In a way, how I saw my father was how I saw God: a figure of authority that wasn't interested in me. How wrong was I!

When I became a Christian, I realised that God was a real father, one who loved me and wanted the best for me. He's just like the father in the story of the prodigal son. That parable has always been my favourite. I love the picture of the father running towards his son, who has seriously let him down, just to hug and forgive him. God wasn't remote; he was a loving dad. He was also a father who, by sending his son to die on a cross, had given up everything for me. I now 'father' a whole load of guys, but back in my early life, I needed my own earthly models to follow. And sure enough God provided.

Ron was a disabled Second World War veteran who lived on my beat when I was a police officer in Chiswick in the early eighties. Ron had been an observer in the army, but had been shot out of a tree, leaving him with only one good leg. We became firm friends and he doted on Nicole. Often whilst on duty I would pop into his house to be 'fathered'. Ron died shortly after I left the police, but I will never forget his friendship. He always had time for me and never seemed to dwell on his own health problems, though I knew they were serious.

One day I found Ron in terrible pain; by now he had invasive cancer and had had both legs amputated. He too was a Christian, but on this particular day he was angry with God. He said, 'Alan, why has God done this to me?' It wasn't like him at all. I was completely thrown. We prayed together, and I was reminded of the picture of Jesus calming the storm. I shared this with him, not knowing what else to do. His pain disappeared, and he grinned at me. He had been truly touched by God. I guess sometimes even those who are fathers to others need fathering themselves.

Going back to my own dad, I realised as I grew older that being a father is hard. He was just doing his best, as indeed I have tried to do for my own children. None of us are perfect parents. I think in hindsight, like millions of other dads, my own father just struggled to be the dad I needed. When my son, James, was born, I told him that I would always be there for him; I don't think he quite took it in at two weeks old, but that didn't stop me doing the same with my daughter, Jessica. I think intent is everything, even if our execution is sometimes off.

In the last year of my father's life, when he was suffering with Parkinson's disease, I had the sheer joy of taking him to see Bournemouth play West Ham. Yes, *I* took *him*! He didn't say anything, but I don't think this was lost on him. I think he knew I was trying to repair something from the past. As he talked excitedly about his own memories of going to the ground as a young man, there seemed to be a tear in his eye – or maybe it was in mine.

Some months later, just before he died, he grabbed a nurse by the hand, pointed at me and said, 'This is my son. He is a good lad.' I had waited all my life to hear that, but it was worth the wait.

We all have a father waiting to say just that: 'Here is my son, here is my daughter, and you are the apple of my eye.'

God is a great father. He's a brilliant father.
It's his love that's ferocious.

Chapter Ten
Coffee Shops and Getting to Know Your Wife

I've been loving you, loving you day after day.
After all this time, my loving eyes still see you the same.
Don't know what I'd do, what I'd do if you were gone.
I've been loving you, loving you too long.
I'm still falling like the very first time.
I can't believe I still call you mine.
If you walked away, I'd still feel this way.
The Shires, 'Loving You Too Long'

Some years ago, Nicole and I were having a meal with a couple who were looking to join our church. The conversation got onto the challenges and pressures of marriage. We, like them, had been together for over a quarter of a century. The husband asked me whether we ever rowed. Presumably he thought that church leaders were too saintly to get into arguments. I told him that once I had got so angry that I picked up a plate of cottage pie (my favourite meal) and threw it on the floor.

I quickly added that I was ashamed of my behaviour (I have never since repeated this stupidity). But things like that happen in the heat of the moment. The husband asked me how long ago this had happened. 'Well, actually, it was last week,' I rather shamefully replied. The look of shock on their faces was priceless. They thought that we lived in a state of unwavering matrimonial bliss. Happily, this couple ultimately decided to join our church because we were the first church leaders who had been completely honest with them about such issues.

It is difficult to help others when you are not honest with yourself. I have seen far too many seemingly stable marriages fall apart. Nicole and I have a great marriage, and we are often asked to help those in marital difficulty, but our own relationship has grown and matured over time. We have had to contend with many struggles and difficulties which, when we set off on our lives together, we were unprepared for. We got married on the hottest day of 1984; in that perfect weather we probably looked like a dream couple, without a care in the world. But appearances can be deceptive. We both had issues. Nicole was from a very difficult background, and I came from a family that never showed any emotion. Our only preparation for married life was a talk with our vicar, who warned us how uncomfortable sex was for wives. That went down a real treat!

Of course, nothing can fully prepare you for life as a couple. Family issues, money pressures, career responsibilities... all while getting used to the idea of living together for the rest of your lives. And that's before kids arrive! So despite our newfound faith in God, we struggled to hold it together – so much so that twenty years ago we could easily have gone our separate ways.

But we didn't. Instead we dug deep, put the effort in

and started making an effort to go to coffee shops and talk. We found that we didn't know each other as well as we thought. We began to do other things too – like booking holidays without the kids, having date nights and so on. In truth, we rebuilt our marriage from the ground up, and this time it was built to last. Folks in our church often asked me about our afternoons in Caffè Nero. The answer was simple: we were investing in our marriage.

I remember one particular occasion picking Nicole up from her staff Christmas function. As I walked in, a rather drunken guy grabbed me. 'There are some gorgeous women in there,' he said, rather inappropriately. 'Especially that one.' He pointed to Nicole. I watched her dancing and felt a deep sense of joy. I heard God speaking to me. I realised we were back on track, and that despite our difficulties she was, and always will be, my soul mate.

God puts us together and he keeps us from falling apart. But sadly the divorce rate amongst Christians is almost the same as for non-Christians. I don't think the church prepares its young people adequately for marriage.

As a pastor, along with Nicole, I am often called upon to help couples going through marital difficulties. I share with them the honest truth. We struggled too. But nevertheless, we had made it through, and with God's help so will they.

God gets it, because he loves marriage.

He invented it.

Chapter Eleven
Cleaning the Gravestones
or Reaching the Nations

In that day you will say: 'Give praise to the LORD,
proclaim his name; make known among the nations
what he has done, and proclaim that his name is exalted.
Isaiah Twelve

When the well dressed man on my doorstep told me that he had come to collect money to, and I quote, 'clean up the gravestones', I couldn't help but smile.

'It's on behalf of the local church,' he said with a sickly smile. 'It's not that we want to collect a huge amount, just fifteen hundred pounds. With that we can clean the ones that have deteriorated, and make everything look nice. The church is important, you know. It does weddings and funerals.'

At this point, I started to laugh, thinking of the money our church had raised that year for a very different reason.

Back in 2006, there were just forty of us in our church in Buxton, but we had a dream to open a coffee shop right in the middle of town. The idea was that it would serve as an open door to the church. More than that, we planned to send money from its revenue to a church in

Clarens, South Africa. They needed money for their school and their many ongoing projects helping the poor.

Now, none of us were flush with money, nothing like the amounts we needed, anyway. But with the determined leadership of our minister, Tim Davies, money kept pouring in. One day someone even posted a cheque for eighty thousand pounds. We never discovered who it was from. God kept turning up and money kept flowing in. We never took out a loan, though it was tempting. Every time we thought about it, God seemed to tell us not to. In fact on one occasion I was all for getting a business loan, but the words came back: 'No fetters, no conditions, trust God'. So that's what we did.

We spotted a building right in the centre of town. It was an old bank and had recently been used – and slightly abused – as a furniture shop and then a restaurant. The price was four hundred thousand pounds. Miraculously, by this stage we had three hundred thousand, so that is what we offered. The offer was firmly declined. But the very next day the owners went into liquidation, and we got a call from the bank. They told us we could have it for our offer. Wow!

Of course, that was just the start of our journey. To buy the building was one thing; to sort out all its problems and refit it as a coffee shop was quite another. If we had needed faith to buy the building, we needed even more to turn it into a successful business. It takes a lot of people to start a business like that: someone to put in the miles of electric cable, someone to build the furniture, someone to project manage the whole scheme, someone to put in a bespoke counter... But the miracles just kept coming. People appeared from nowhere to help us, and every time we thought the money had run out, along came God and more flowed in. Always just enough.

When it was completed, the coffee shop was simply fabulous. Everything was top quality. We even had a lift and two downstairs toilets. More importantly, money started to flow to our friends in Clarens, money for the school toilets, money for the church building, money for their outreach project to the poor, and money for farming projects. And guess what? I got to go to Africa. In fact, I made three memorable trips, sometimes just observing, sometimes preaching and sharing.

It was a remarkable experience. I met some wonderful people, like Samuel and Topsy, a couple my age who lived and breathed Jesus. They were pillars of their local community, and Samuel led worship at the church. He put on quite the show, playing keyboard and jumping with joy across the stage. I also met Justice, a huge tower of a man who, many years before, while still an atheist (in fact, deeply into witchcraft), had had a vivid dream telling him to go to the Clarens church. He tried to resist, but he kept getting the same dream. Then one day he walked into the church, discovered Jesus and never left. By the time I met him, he was a church leader.

And it didn't stop with Clarens. Their little church reached out to those around it, beginning to plant churches in places like the nearby city of Maseru. They truly touched their local community, with many coming to their conferences and becoming followers of Jesus. My time there was like going to one long party – sheer unending joy. I had a ball.

But someone had to manage that coffee shop, and for a time that person was me, along with a talented and charismatic friend. It was a tough learning experience for us both. But again people turned up to help us – so many, in fact, that we even had to send volunteers away. And Buxton itself responded. Our coffee shop became the town's busiest, eventually causing Costa to try and buy us out. But this was our church and our community coffee shop, and we weren't selling to anyone.

Soon we began to employ a team to run things. Many people filled those important roles over the years, some coming back into employment for the first time in years, others working their way out of depression or poverty. Many became christians.

There were many incredible stories. One customer came in every day; she was dying from cancer and feeling lonely. The staff always supported her, giving her free drinks and food. They let her lie on our pristine leather sofa. When she died they attended her funeral. You don't get that in Costa.

A close friend of mine, Steve, who was a senior director in the NHS, came to visit the cafe one day. I wasn't around, so he sat there drinking coffee for a couple of hours. Steve was an agnostic, but that evening he phoned me to say that, sitting there on the sofa, watching people come and go, he had had what he described as a spiritual experience. So profound was it that he had felt unable to speak. He described it as a deep sense of peace and the feeling of a presence. I knew who this was.

We had additional space above the coffee shop, and this housed a debt counselling service, a pregnancy advice service and our church office. My day as a church leader started with the best cappuccino you could buy in town! That was cool. Many years later, the coffee shop is still churning out cappuccinos and is still the church door into the town.

You see, God does stuff on a grand scale. To him, fifteen hundred pounds, even six hundred thousand pounds is nothing. He uses his church, changes lives and reaches the nations.

By the way, the Buxton gravestones never did get their refresh.

Shame.

Chapter Twelve
God Bless Gary Neville

No harm will over take you, no disaster will come near your tent. For he will command his angels concerning you to guard you in all your ways; they will lift up their hands so that you will not strike your foot against a stone.
Psalm Ninety One

Robin has always been one of my very best friends. He's just a great guy. He has a few issues he has had to deal with, including some physical limitations and various other restrictions. But he lives life to the full and has two great parents who, over the years, have fought for him to live an independent and full life.

Robin always surprises and he always shines. When we set up the coffee shop in Buxton, some people told me that Robin really shouldn't be front of house, that he couldn't cope with multiple customers. I have never liked the word 'shouldn't'. I decided that they were talking nonsense. I took him on as my top barista. Robin vindicated my faith. He was a star. People loved his out there sense of humour and, of course, his excellent coffee.

Each morning at the coffee shop we started with a

prayer that included everyone, even if they didn't go to church – it's just what we did. I was somewhat surprised that Robin insisted on finishing every prayer session with the statement 'God bless Gary Neville'. I asked Robin why we needed to pray for Gary Neville every day. Now, Robin is a Manchester United fan, and his answer was simple: 'He's our captain.' That seemed perfectly good to me. Over time I found myself praying for Gary Neville every day.

Robin was a great help to me. One day, a number of staff let me down. Robin heard, and at seven in the morning on his day off, he got on a bus to come and help me. When I asked him why, he just said, 'Mate, I knew you needed me.' That was Robin: a top man and one of the best Christians I know.

Some years after that incident, Robin's mum, Joan, asked to speak to me. Robin was meant to be going into routine respite care to give his parents a break. He had done this many times before, but this time he seemed to be very upset and afraid. In the end his psychologist found out why. Many years earlier, as a young teen, Robin had entered a respite facility in Chesterfield and had been physically and mentally abused. At one point he had been strapped down to a bed. It was horrendous. Robin had held all this in for years, not wanting to, as he saw it, 'let anyone down'. We were all stunned.

I pondered long and hard as to how I could help my dear friend, and eventually I came up with an idea. I thought that if we both went back to where all this had happened, then perhaps Robin could get some closure. His parents (who, of course, had immediately got in touch with the authorities) felt it was worth a try.

And so, on a sunny Peak District day, Robin and I drove to Chesterfield. By now the decrepit old hospital had been knocked down, and in its place was a fabulous block of flats for the elderly. We sat talking in the gardens, which were beautiful, but I could feel that Robin was very upset. Then a miracle happened. Two old ladies who lived in the flats approached us and asked why we were there. Robin, being Robin, told them. I just watched as a remarkable scene unfolded before me: the two kindly old ladies hugged Robin and told him not to be afraid anymore. They said that this was their home now, and a place of peace and love. Robin was never to let what had happened to him define his life. He was completely free of the past.

It was quite remarkable. Some might say that those two women just happened to be passing, that God didn't send them. I have to disagree. In a lifetime as a Christian, I've seen too many of these 'coincidences'. Now, I don't know if I have ever met angels, but if not, these two lovely women were surely the nearest thing. A big smile spread across Robin's face. We decided to pray. We thanked God for the healing and told him we trusted him for the future. I knew that Robin wasn't totally healed, but the long journey had more than begun. A light had shone and darkness was fast disappearing.

At the end of our prayers, I heard myself say those immortal words: 'And, God, please bless Gary Neville.'

I'm sure he will.

God loves Gary Neville.

Chapter Thirteen
'Thank You' – The Most Powerful Words I Know

Appreciation can make a day – even change a life.
Your willingness to put it into words is all that is necessary.
Margaret Cousins

My grandchildren asked me if I was a hero. I said no way, but I told them I was surrounded by heroes.
Lieutenant Richard Winters, 'Easy Company', speaking in 2005

This evening I spent time with a new church leader. He was young and enthusiastic, and he wanted to know something of my experience of leadership, both in the secular world and in a church environment. I wanted to focus on humility and what people these days call 'servant leadership'. But my problem is that, when I think of leaders telling others how to be humble, I get overly cynical. It's probably because I have seen so many people fall from grace. Indeed, the author of my favourite Christian book on humility was forced to leave his leadership role because it turned out he was a bit of a bully.

An old friend of mine and I used to take the mickey out of all this stuff. We would sit at the back of a church leadership seminar on humility and come up with titles for our own books on the subject: *Humility Is Us* or *Discover How To Be Truly Humble Like What We Are.* You get the drift.

Given my cynicism, I struggled to come up with an answer to this young man's questions. But then I thought about my favourite TV series, *Band of Brothers.*

There is one scene in particular which has always resonated with me. It involves a conversation between a sergeant and a lieutenant of the heroic Easy Company. The sergeant has endured a torrid time. He has lost many close friends and has had to endure serving under a weak and disgraced leader. Throughout, he has maintained an impeccably professional attitude, showing his men the leadership, encouragement and, indeed, kindness that his commanding officer fails to exhibit. In this particular scene, the lieutenant movingly remarks that, despite all that Easy Company have faced, it has always had a leader, one who showed strength, determination, coolness, humour and integrity.

It always makes me well up.

Although I have received more than my fair share of encouragement over the years, I can also think of times in my life when I have felt utterly ignored. It's something that happens to us all at some point.

Take, for instance, when I was working in the NHS. I spent two years pushing for a new hospital in the West Midlands. My team's hard work ultimately paid off, and the new hospital was finally built, but it sometimes felt like we had to take on every political party and professional group along the way. I left my job as CEO of the new hospital just four months prior to the royal opening. Everybody expected me to get an invitation to meet Princess Anne at this opening, but it never came. Indeed, I was later told that the new CEO, when asked by her royal highness about the work that had gone into the project, told her that it was all down to him and his team!

And in my experience, church leadership is often just as thankless – sometimes even far more so – than the secular world. The reality is that some Church leaders can be particularly blind to the feelings of those around them, especially their own team. So often they fail to say thank you. Sadly, the truth is that I have collected far more stories to this effect from those in the church than in all of my secular work life.

Many years ago, I attended a leaving do for someone who for years I had worked with in a church. I had covered his back many times. It wasn't that in his farewell speech he didn't thank me, or even mention my name, so much as the fact that he didn't thank anyone. Not one person. It left a deep, long-lasting scar on those who had supported him all this time.

But the problem with all this is that I am thinking solely of the times when *I* have been unappreciated, when *I* have been taken for granted. You may be doing the same. But surely I have done the same to others? I can't particularly remember doing so, but the people I have mentioned probably didn't have a clue what they had done either. You see, on this issue we are all completely undone.

There is only one person who gets all this completely right. Jesus was the king of kings. The Bible tells us that he was the absolute reflection of God. But he came down to our level, to our world and suffered profoundly. He was poor. He never owned anything or married. He was forever ridiculed and attacked. He was rarely honoured or thanked. Jesus was let down by his friends and family, scorned by the authorities and ultimately tortured and crucified. Yet he never failed to show love to those around him. He reached out to the unwanted. He washed his disciples' feet. He forgave those who had placed him on the cross, and he even saved a robber who was being crucified next to him.

The Bible says of him that he would not shout or cry out or raise his voice in the streets. He would not even break a bruised reed or snuff out a smouldering wick. Yet he would still be God's chosen servant, one whom God had chosen, and one whom God would delight in.

So why should I be surprised when people let me down? Why should I feel like I have been the victim? The fact is that, compared to Jesus' grace, we just don't cut it – not one of us. And instead of dwelling on my misfortunes, I could spend more time being concerned for those I have let down, those I have ignored or failed to thank. They are out there somewhere, I just know.

Jesus taught us to love those around us, to put them first – not ourselves and our own self gain. I can follow someone like that.

So, back to my discussions with the new and enthusiastic church leader. I urged him to be aware of the team around him, to nurture and support them. I implored him to remember that a word of encouragement, a word of thanks, can lift people's hearts; in fact, it can move mountains. I told him that if he wanted to be a great leader, he would need to understand that his two most powerful words are 'thank you'.

I also recounted the scene from *Band of Brothers*, which finishes like this: when the lieutenant has praised the sergeant and all that he has done for his men, he pauses, grins and then says, 'And, sergeant, you have got no idea who I am talking about, do you?'

Now that's humility worth having.

Chapter Fourteen
'Ta Ta' Just Won't Cut It

I cannot help noticing that at moments of national crisis even secular icons like the New York Times *open their editorial pages to priests, rabbis and pastors. Atheists and evolutionary psychologists maintain a discreet silence, for good reason. What words or comfort might they offer?*
Philip Yancey

A close friend of mine who is a church pastor was once asked to conduct a Humanist funeral. The family fiercely specified that there be no mention of religion of any kind. 'Sure thing,' he said. 'Leave it all to me.' When the day of the funeral arrived, he said a few brief words by way of introduction, pressed the button for the body to go on its way, and shouted 'Ta Ta then!'

The family were appalled and demanded to know why the pastor had said nothing remotely spiritual or encouraging. 'But you said you didn't want any of that,' he replied. 'You told me you didn't believe in any of that stuff.'

I thought it was funny; after all, he had only given them what they had really wanted. But I also wondered if their sense of injustice revealed something deep within even the most atheistic of human hearts. When it comes down to it, only Jesus has the answer when that final day comes.

Tony Footitt was one of my very best friends. I met Tony towards the end of my NHS career, when I spent a number of years working one day per week with Nottinghamshire Healthcare as a management consultant. Tony, like me, was a long in the tooth professional who had seen most things the NHS could throw at you. He was fiercely proud of the NHS, and he had a wicked sense of humour. I guess that's why we clicked.

Tony was incredibly kind and gentle, but you crossed him at your peril. I remember a new director starting his first day in the trust and noisily pacing up and down outside the boardroom, waiting for Tony and his team to finish their meeting. Tony saw him waiting and asked who he was. 'I am the new director,' came the reply, 'and I am waiting to enter this room.'

Tony's response was what I fondly came to know as 'classic Tony': 'I don't care who you are, but please stop pacing the floor and upsetting my staff.'

Over time, Tony and I became very close friends. Though we worked hard, we always found time for a chat and some lunch. Famously, Tony once got us both completely lost in a wing of Rampton Hospital designed for the most violent of patients. That was scary. He also got us arrested one night, as we wandered around the perimeter of Rampton discussing a board meeting and inadvertently walked into a high security area.

But Tony had a problem, one that he shared with me from the very start. He had prostate cancer. He had chosen radiotherapy when he had had the chance to have the prostate removed surgically, and he feared he had made the wrong choice. As time went on, Tony appeared more and more worried. He tried countless different new drugs, but to no avail.

Tony wasn't a committed Christian, but if ever there was a model Christian, it was him. He was considerate to others, always backed the underdog, and had a grace and kindness that won over the most difficult of individuals. Tony always seemed to know your deepest needs. For example, in my new job, I missed a simple thing: the staff Christmas lunch at my old place of work. Tony guessed that this might be an issue for me, and every Christmas his staff lunch was without fail switched to whatever day I was in the trust, simply so I could come. That was Tony.

As time went on, Tony's illness progressed, and I realised that he might not make it through. Our discussions became more meaningful, and we often talked about my faith. The trust had a strict policy of political correctness, meaning that no one was allowed to share their faith at work. But politically incorrect as I am, I prayed with him anyway, sometimes walking together in the car park so no one would complain.

One day, I received a phone call and was told that Tony had collapsed. He had suffered a stroke brought on by all the cancer drugs. He had specified that, in such an eventuality, only his family, Mike (our excellent CEO) and I were to see him. My visit was desperately sad. Tony could hardly move, struggling to get his hand into mine to say hello. I just held his hand and talked to him like I always did. I didn't ask him to formally accept Jesus into his life, to say a prayer or anything like that. It just felt important for me to hold his hand. I knew that all I needed to say had been said already. And I knew that Jesus was there.

Tony died, but here's the thing: for all its political correctness, this close NHS community had no idea how to respond. As I talked to many of the lovely staff affected by Tony death (all of them atheists or agnostics), I realised they had no answer, no solace, no comfort. A few months after Tony's passing, staff gathered at his grave to remember him. I hadn't expected to say anything, but after a few moments of quiet reflection, I felt a number of eyes looking at me. I realised why. They knew I was a Christian; they knew I would have something to say. I can't quite remember exactly what I did say, but it was something along the lines of that every bone in my body told me that Tony knew Jesus, and that he was with him in glory.

You see, I think it goes something like this: many people resist Jesus; they find any number of reasons not to accept his truth. But deep down in every person, deep down in every soul, is an emptiness that can only be filled by him. At every funeral I have been to since, the same thought comes: 'Ta Ta' just won't cut it.

Only Jesus will do.

Chapter Fifteen
The Church Turns Up – Big Style

Through the fire and the flood, I know that I am loved.
I can hear you singing over me.
I hear your melody. I hear your symphony.
There's nothing louder than the sound of my father.
Urban Rescue, 'Song of My Father'

There is no pain in our lives that eclipses the death of a loved one, particularly when the death comes early, far too early. The pain, the outpouring of grief, the pure sadness is overwhelming even as a Christian.

On the day that Michelle and her husband, Steve, called me to say they had some news, I feared the worst. Michele had been facing cancer for some time. That day she and Steve had travelled to Birmingham to see Michelle's consultant for a prognosis following an extensive course of chemotherapy. The treatment had afforded her a short period of hope, but it had not been enough.

As a church pastor, I had got to know this vibrant and warm hearted couple. Michelle was a talented and bubbly TV personality and reporter, with a beautiful smile. Steve was a brilliant, determined business man. They were the sort of people everyone wanted to be around, generating fun and energy wherever they went. And they had two young children, who were both on my mind as I knocked on their door.

Steve met me at the door. 'Alan, we have decided to stop the treatment. We know Michelle hasn't got long. But the time we have is precious, and this decision gives us quality time with our children.'

My heart sank. I prayed for them both, of course, but sometimes prayers feel like you are whispering to God in the dark. That's how it was that day. But you know what? Miracles happened anyway. People visited, taking Michelle out to Chatsworth House, always one of her favourites; they cooked daily for the family; they sent gifts and they turned up to clean. A curry club was even started to give Steve something to look forward to.

And then there was the carol service. It was Christmas, but Michelle was too weak to come to church. So we brought the carol service to her lounge! A local brass band was invited, and we sang carols and read lessons. Most of Buxton heard our musical extravaganza that day! We were all emotionally wrecked, but we had purpose, boy did we have purpose. It was just magical. I remember thinking that we literally touched heaven that night.

Michelle died a few days later. Steve told me that, when he went into her bedroom to draw the curtains back, he saw the most stunning sunrise. He felt God was speaking to him. I believed him. He turned up at church the next week to thank us for helping them through such a difficult time. Not that the help was to stop there, of course.

There are times when a church mucks up. I ought to know. I have seen it myself enough times. But sometimes, when a church rises up as one, with purpose and intent, it can be flipping awesome. I mean, where else can an eclectic group of dysfunctional, flawed people work together as one, with compassion and commitment driven by a higher love and belief? I can't think of anywhere. Only the church. It's God's church. It's his plan, his only plan and sometimes, when we remember what we are about, it works like it was always meant to. Jesus said that nothing would ever stop his church here on earth. And it won't. If you are reading this and think that the church is dead, think again. It's going to outlast and outlive everything because it belongs to him.

He has the last word.

Chapter Sixteen
I Have Bad Depression:
the Dying Seagull

Depression is the wrong word. The word depression makes me think of a flat tyre, something punctured and unmoving. Depression laced with terror is not something flat or still.
Matt Haig, *Reasons to Stay Alive*

At the root of this dilemma is the way we view mental health in this country. Whether an illness affects your heart, your leg or your brain, it's still an illness and there should be no distinction.
Michelle Obama

A friend of mine once challenged me to find a picture to represent what it feels like to be deeply depressed and this is it. I once saw a majestic-looking seagull struggling to regain its footing on some rocks at the edge of the shore. It was badly injured. The sea was fast approaching, and as the waves lapped ever higher against the rocks, the seagull desperately struggled to lift itself out of reach of the water. It was a futile cause. That to me is deep depression. A feeling that things are completely hopeless, and no hope whatsoever on the horizon.

Steve, a dear friend of mine from university, suffered terribly from depression, and he once described it to me as like being in a dark and desperate place but having nowhere else you would prefer to be. Think about that one. He died having consumed so much alcohol he choked on his own vomit. Steve was kind, funny, highly intelligent and gifted, but like many young men today he lost his struggle far too young – at just twenty one.

I had never really struggled with depression, but at the age of fifty five it hit me like a mighty wave. I am not completely sure about the cause, but I do now know it wasn't my fault.

In the summer of 2016, Nicole and I moved from our lovely Peak District home to the centre of Manchester, taking on an unpaid role supporting five churches, and in particular assisting a young couple leading a church full of university students. It seemed a dream move. We felt like we had done all we could with the church in Buxton. We were excited and confident that God had pointed us to this new opportunity.

We loved our new church, and they seemed to love us. But I missed our old home, our old community. In contrast to the beauty of the Peak District, Manchester seemed cold, grey, a world where people rushed about their business without time to stop and talk. There were no hills, no open places to walk, no greenery at all.

And then I discovered that our new role was a good deal less substantial than I was used to. We had moved into the centre assuming that we needed to be situated in the very hub of the city. But the majority of the church lived in the suburbs. One colleague unhelpfully confided that they themselves would never have moved to the centre.

It got worse. We found that we had innumerable problems with our new flat. You name it, we had it. It flooded several times, we had legal disputes, parking disputes, faulty appliances, faulty windows, faulty everything. Even the stuff we ordered to replace our lost possessions got lost or destroyed on the way. We actually counted forty three things that went wrong. It seemed like more than just bad luck.

Maybe in different circumstances, I could have coped, but for whatever reason I didn't. Some close friends have since told me that they worried about the toll my church pastoring had taken. They reckoned I had been drained, sucked dry. Nicole also felt that my depression had started much earlier than our move. I don't know if any of that's true myself, but I do know that in that moment I felt utterly powerless to cope with what was being thrown at us. Whatever the cause, things got very dark.

I started to feel physically ill. My stomach felt permanently knotted. I had panic attacks. I struggled to enjoy anything. And I began to feel really guilty. I had dragged Nicole away from her job. We had left friends. We had left our church. We had sold our lovely home and bought a problem property. We were in our mid fifties – this wasn't the time to be making these kinds of mistakes.

I started to wonder if I had misheard God. How could he want us to go through this?

Things got worse. I was encouraged to go to the local surgery and ask for antidepressants. The doctor had an aggressive and seemingly uncaring attitude. He put me on antidepressants from the medicine group called selective serotonin reuptake inhibitors (SSRIs) – but on a huge dose. His attitude seemed to be 'Well, if you want them, you can have them big time'.

It was then that my problems really started. For whatever reason I reacted very badly to the drug. It was only much later that I discovered that I was the victim of a side effect that only about one percent of the population suffer when they are prescribed SSRIs. I had severe drug toxicity, which essentially means that you are slowly being poisoned and your body is closing down. But no one realised.*

In less than two weeks, I went from mildly depressed to seriously suicidal. I quickly developed psychotic depression, which means hallucinations and delusional thinking. At first I couldn't settle at all, and would pace relentlessly around our flat. Then I lost all my energy and could hardly get up at all. I retreated to bed whenever I could. I began to see strange things whirling around in my room. I honestly thought that the police were watching me, that at any moment I would be arrested. I couldn't laugh. In fact, I went months without even a smile. Sometimes I forgot where I was and who I was. I developed a tremor so bad that I couldn't even put my cash card into a machine or hold a cup of coffee. I ground my teeth at night, my muscles ached, my stomach bloated, I had trouble swallowing, I couldn't sleep. I had suicidal thoughts. I felt that I had lost my faith. Above all, I felt utterly and deeply ashamed of my weakness.

They say that antidepressants stop the mind from dancing. In my case, they brought my every sense to a crashing halt.

I was no longer the man I used to be, not in any shape or form. I had to stop helping the Manchester church. I was referred to the local mental health team, but they just prescribed more drugs. They should have spotted that I was having a severe reaction, but they didn't. It all happened so quickly, it was horrific. When you have very bad depression, you suffer a triple whammy. Firstly, you feel lost. Secondly, no one has any idea how you feel – after all, it's not like they can see a broken body, or the obvious physical symptoms that come with other diseases. And finally, not only do some people not get it, but often they actually treat you with indifference, even anger. They think it's your fault.

Let me give a few examples. A long standing colleague, a caring and decent man in most respects, told me that my problem was that I didn't have enough faith. He informed me that I had not faced many difficulties in my life and I needed to toughen up. It was absolute nonsense, but because I was so low I believed it all. This is a common trait amongst sufferers: their already low self-esteem leads them to believe any criticism must be right. One of my friends stopped calling or communicating with me altogether. He later confessed that for years he had relied on me as a counsellor, and that he just couldn't cope with the fact I was so ill. A close friend broke down in front of me and told me, 'You look like shit.' That was painful. Another church leader, who I had helped multiple times, never contacted me again.

There were other more distressing reactions, like someone who had always remembered my birthday deciding not to send me a card. Or people who regularly asked us to their parties striking us off the list, on what basis I don't know. Then there were people who sadly just didn't respond at all. My most painful experience was to hear Nicole phoning one of our old churches in tears, desperately asking for them to help. No help came.

If I had had a heart attack or cancer, they would undoubtedly have kept in touch. I don't seek to blame anyone here. They are all good people. I understand that they just may not have been able to cope themselves. I am just saying it how it was. I have spoken to countless other sufferers since and this is a common theme. At a time when they were ill, really ill, they felt abandoned ignored and even blamed. Why is mental health treated so differently?

Many figures in the Bible appear to have suffered with depression. Job is one of the best known. He lost all he had worked for, but despite his unhelpful friends he trusted in God, even though God never actually explains to him why he allowed such suffering. Peter, also, must have been severely depressed once he realised he had let Jesus down. Paul's life does not appear to have been a bundle of laughs, and his writings give a clear indication of depression. Then there was Elijah, who ran away to die even after a monumental victory. The Bible tells us that he sat next to a broom tree and prayed that he might die. He said, 'I have had enough, Lord. Take my life. I am no better than my ancestors.' Jonah, too, got so down he felt it might be better for him to die. Then there was Moses, who at times felt like he had been betrayed by his own people. And Jeremiah, who wrestled with great loneliness and feelings of defeat and insecurity. Then there is Hannah, who grieved about her own situation to the point of almost total despair.

And, of course, there is Jesus himself, who in the garden of Gethsemane said, 'My soul is overwhelmed with sorrow to the point of death.'

If as Christians we are not meant to suffer depression, why is the Bible full of people who have gone through exactly that? As Christians, are we immune from mental health issues? Should we, the Christians, never get Alzheimer's disease? Are our minds somehow mysteriously protected? No! It all gets us just as it gets everyone else. So here are some facts. Christians get depressed. Christians have major breakdowns. Christians suffer terrible reactions to drugs and Christians commit suicide. And it isn't their fault anymore than someone who gets cancer or has a heart attack. They are just ill.

Michelle Obama is right. It is time to change our thinking. The dying seagull needed help, not just observation.

* For a more in depth understanding of the dangers of SSRI's, read *The Pill That Steals Lives*, an excellent and heart rending testimony by Katinka Blackford Newman, who experienced much of what I did.

N.B If you are reading this book and are on antidepressants, I would make the obvious point: don't stop taking them without your doctor's advice.

Chapter Seventeen
I Have Bad Depression: the Problem of Pain

But whilst Joseph was there in prison, the lord was with him.
Genesis Thirty Nine

I am no victim, I live with a vision.
I'm covered by the force of love, covered in my saviour's blood.
Kristine DiMarco, 'I Am No Victim'

One of the things I have thought about a lot this last year through my depression and illness is that old chestnut. Why does God allow pain? I know that there are millions of people who have suffered far more than me, but this time it was personal. Why did I have such a bad time, why did I get severe depression? Why did I suffer such a reaction to the drugs? What had I done to deserve it?

Rachael and Martin are two friends of mine who have done remarkable things for the church in the UK both as youth leaders and pastors. About eight years ago, for a short time, they became something of a national focus as tragically their thirteen year old son, Sam, was killed by a driver who mounted the pavement, ran over him and then drove away without stopping, thus provoking a nationwide hunt. What was stunning was the grace and serenity of Martin and Rachael when questioned by the media. They showed only love and compassion towards the perpetrator who by now was in police custody. They explained that though they were grief stricken they were also Christians who followed Jesus Christ and they could only forgive. It was remarkable and for a few precious moments shook our cynical media to the core.

Just recently I heard that Rachael is now battling a serious illness. Momentarily I got angry and asked God a few straight questions. Why her Lord? Surely she and Martin have gone through enough? How can you allow this? After all, they work for you! I am now nearing sixty and, as such, have seen a fair amount of pain and suffering, but this one just seemed to be beyond belief. So let me answer this question for Rachael and Martin, and indeed me, along with the millions who suffer today.

Firstly, I know that God is good all the time. That may sound a simple statement but it is fundamental in this debate. If we start to believe the lies that he isn't good then I think we descend into a dark and bitter world. One where our God is not really God anymore. One where cynicism and ultimately non-belief grow like a cancer. Some people tell me that they don't recognise such a God in the Old Testament, but they are wrong. If you read it properly it tells you of a loving father who does everything for his children. The children rebel and he still loves them. Yes, he punishes them, but only for their own good, constantly urging them to return and come back to his loving arms. He then gives them something even better by sending Jesus. That's the God I follow.

You see, I know God is good. I know it because he says he is good and I trust him. I know it because he sent his one and only son to die for our sins and shame, and I have a lot of that stuff. I know it because all the good that I have comes from him. I know it because he has given me joy and happiness. I know it because he was there at the beginning and he will see me through to the next stage. I know it because in my darkest hour I still knew he was there even when I didn't like him. I know it because Rachael and Martin are still worshipping him and they are smart, cool people. I know it because even as I write, the very bricks that make up my house are shouting it out. I just know and that's enough for me.

Secondly, I don't blame him for anything. He didn't create a fallen world with sin and death. The original world he created was perfect with no pain. We screwed it up. Sometimes people tell me that when they get to heaven they will join the queue for people who want to challenge God about all this. I don't think any such queue exists. He is God. He is perfect. If there was such a queue then he wouldn't be perfect and he wouldn't be God. There are things I don't understand but then I am not God, *he is.*

Thirdly, I believe that he can use any situation for good. In fact I would go further than that. I believe that God wants to prosper us and do us good. Let me go back to my own pain. I was terribly depressed and very ill. I still don't know why, but I do know that God is using what I went through for good. So, here are some things that have enhanced my life and others through the hell I went through.

He restored some relationships and strengthened others. I had not seen my sister and her family as much as we both would have wanted, but now I do. Furthermore some of the friends who couldn't cope with my illness have since been very honest with me, and through that honesty our friendship has been enhanced. Secondly, in the middle of it all, God sent some new friends. Ken and Sandy happened to have moved to Manchester at the same time. We were introduced. We quickly became friends and when I got ill it was as if God had sent two angels to help, sustain and encourage us. They came round every week to pray and have communion. I couldn't speak, but they kept coming. They thought I just never spoke. Now they can't understand why they can never shut me up!

One other benefit was that I have understood mental illness for the first time, which is ironic as I have previously counselled loads of people who have depression, in my church role. Many more people now cross my door because they know I get it.

Finally, I believe that whatever we face God has beaten it by sending Jesus to die on a cross so that we might have life in all its fullness, which means that if we trust him we are going to heaven. This world isn't it. He stuffed depression, he hammered all illness, he defeated death, and he smashed our sin. In fact the cross, which is an affront to so many, sets us free completely. I am not a victim, I am blessed and even if I had died, however tragic for my friends and family, the final outcome would have been the same. I would be with him in heaven. Life would have got me, not death.

I have always been struck by a song by Matt Maher. It's about a man who questions God. Why have you put me through this? Where were you? Where were you in all my pain? The stark answer comes back: 'I was on the cross all alone.' He has done it all.

> Lost,
> Everything is lost,
> And everything I've loved before is gone.
> Alone, like the coming of the frost,
> And a cold winter's chill in my stony heart.
>
> Where were You when all that I've hoped for,
> Where were You when all that I've dreamed
> Came crashing down in shambles around me?
> You were on the cross.
>
> 'You Were On The Cross'
> by Matt Maher from the album *Alive Again*.

A friend of mine once told me that, if a person suffers sea sickness, a good seaman will encourage them to fix their eyes on something in the distance, maybe the sun, maybe a piece of land. Apparently this is the only real cure on a long voyage. When we face deep pain, we must fix our eyes on Jesus, no matter how tumultuous the storm. Paul, who himself knew deep depression and anxiety wrote: 'Let us fix our eyes on Jesus, the author and perfector of our faith, who for the joy set before him endured the cross, scorning its shame.'

If we look up to heaven, beyond our current situation, then we see something magnificent, lasting, and perfect.

We see hope, not despair. We see certainty, not confusion. We see victory, not defeat. Whatever I faced, he was with me every step of the way, even when I couldn't feel it or see it.

One of my my favourite films is *Forrest Gump*, and there is one moment when Lieutenant Dan, having been saved by the hapless Grump, has to have both legs amputated. Lieutenant Dan is angry; he thinks that he was meant to die on the battlefield with honour, just like his brave ancestors, but he will now be forced to live as a paraplegic. Gump has interfered with his destiny. As the two of them tussle underneath a hospital bed, Dan says, 'This wasn't meant to happen, I was Lieutenant Dan Taylor.' Gump, in his wonderfully under stated way, replies, 'But you are still Lieutenant Dan.'

At the end of what was a horrible illness, I often wondered if I would ever be me again. Would I ever be the father, husband, friend, pastor – the Alan that people used to know? But now I get it. My identity is in him. I always was and always will be his son.

And that is sufficient for me.

Chapter Eighteen
I Have Bad Depression: Learning to Fly Again

I know it's all you've got to just be strong,
And it's a fight just to keep it together.
I know you think that you are too far gone.
But hope is never lost.
Hope is never lost.
Hold on, don't let go.
Just take one step closer.
Put one foot in front of the other.
You'll get through this. Just follow the light in the darkness.
You're gonna be OK.
Jenn Johnson, 'Bethel Church'

I have often mused about the apostle Paul's writings on the armour of God. You know the passage: the sword of the spirit, the breastplate of righteousness, the shield of faith, etc. But there is one thing curiously missing from Paul's description: any armour to cover the back–everything else is protected. Theologians tell me that the reason that the back is not protected is that Roman soldiers never turned their backs – they were always attacking – or alternatively, that their backs were covered by fellow soldiers.

Based on my experience of depression, I would suggest a slightly different theory. Simply put, God always covers our backs. He surrounds us all the time. Even when we cannot pick up a sword or a shield, he covers our backs. He certainly covered mine.

There are two specific healing moments from the time of my illness that I particularly recall. The first was a hug from a dear friend. This friend struggles to say to anyone that she is a Christian; she is lovely, but she just doesn't feel good enough. But during one of my lowest points, in a sheer act of love and kindness, she grabbed me in a bear hug and didn't let go for several seconds. Afterwards she told me that, during those brief moments, she had been praying for me. All I know is that I felt a great weight being lifted from me. I think it was a God moment. I had a similar experience when my son James, who sometimes struggles with church stuff, laid his hand on me and prayed for me – wow!

The other moment is more painful to recall. Almost a year later, Nicole and I were walking on our favourite beach in Anglesey. We were talking again about my illness, the sheer darkness and terror of it. Bad memories came flooding back. We argued a bit, I can't even remember what about. As we walked around a cliff and onto some rocks, I slipped, fell and twisted my knee. The physical pain was nothing, but for some reason all the pain and darkness from my illness hit me all over again.

Now I had not cried for two years – not even once throughout the entirety of my illness. This was weird, because normally all it takes is a soppy film to set me off.

In the film *The Holiday*, when Cameron Diaz runs back to Jude Law, I have to pretend I am blowing my nose in case anyone suspects I am blubbing. I even howl in *The Railway Children*, when Jenny Agutter says, 'My Daddy, my Daddy.' But for whatever reason my illness had killed any such expression of these senses. My eyes had remained dry – until that moment.

I lied on the ground and started to cry; in fact, I started to sob uncontrollably. Nicole came and held me, and it all came out. The rotten luck that I had reacted so badly to the drugs. The misery. The shame. The pain I had seen my family go through. The fact that my children had seen me so ill. The comments, the lack of support from some. The waste. The pure futility of it all. I sobbed and sobbed. I thought it would never stop. It was like a never-ending waterfall of emotion, grief and outrage.

But the next day I felt different. A giant weight had been taken from me. It had all bubbled to the surface, and a lot of it had then been washed away. God does that. He's in the business of healing.

Other healing came from living well again. We left Manchester and moved to the magnificent north Wales coast. Walking by the sea. Listening to my favourite composer, Thomas Tallis. Drinking wine in the local Rhos wine shop (the hub of our community). Exploring the magical scenery that is Snowdonia. Walking with friends. Laying a new lawn. Ordering pizza and knowing the sun was right where it should be. One lovely guy from Buxton kindly took me to Mexico for a holiday, even though, looking back, I was still very odd company!

Then there was the local church family. When we moved away from Manchester, I had not lost my faith in

God, but to some extent I had lost my faith in church. It had not been there for me or Nicole when we had needed it most. But then we walked into an independent church set up some years before by a successful business man and a one-time atheist who had found Jesus. It met in a cinema, and it was a bit wild, a bit unconventional, but the people were lovely.

For the first time in years, I felt loved and appreciated by the church – and all this after bearing my soul to them. The more I shared the more they just loved me back. We were invited for dinner, asked to the pub, taken for walks. I discovered Welsh rugby and was made to wear a plastic leek on a night out to watch the local team! One couple, Keith and Alison Fletcher, devoted their Fridays to getting me fit again, taking me walking with their dog, Frank. We were soon joined by others and 'Walks with Frank' was born. The church is magnificent when it does what Jesus tells it to do. Nicole and I were wrapped up in a blanket of love.

I remember attending the men's group for the first time. We met in a cafe. Now I had led lots of men's stuff, and I was confident in talking to guys – that was my scene. But walking in that night I felt afraid and vulnerable. I was worried I might be rejected. I felt out of sorts. I still carried deep scars. But I shouldn't have worried. They welcomed me, shook my hand, gave me dreadful coffee, and listened to my story – even though I had never expected to share it. Then they took me to the pub.

'Is this what you guys normally do?' I sheepishly asked.

'Oh yes,' one of them said. 'All these guys have a

story, tonight it was your turn.'

On my way home, I knew that God had given me one great big bear hug, and I knew for certain that the seagull was going to fly again.

Chapter Nineteen
Speeding Fines

*Jesus was either who he said he was or he was nuts. I
choose to believe he was the son of God.*
Bono

This Jesus stuff is a life changer. It's the promise that
if we repent and follow Jesus then God will forgive
us the bad stuff we have done, deal with death and hell,
and give us eternal life. It's all good. It's the real deal.

And yet some people just don't seem to get it – even
those who identify as Christians. To be blunt, if your idea
of Christianity is once a week going to church to sing
some nice songs, without ever grasping this concept, it's
like going to see your favourite rock star, paying for the
best seat, then spending all your time in the toilet. You
have missed everything.

Once I had to share this life-changing message three
times in a week. Firstly, at the funeral of a beautiful little
girl who had lived a mere three weeks. Secondly, with a
group of impoverished Hindu villagers in South India.
Finally, with a physics student in Manchester. What
struck me that week was that in very different situations
the message is equally relevant and profound. For those

who are grieving and reminded of their own mortality. For those who are poor and in the thrall of a man-made religion. For those who have the highest IQ, but know there is something missing.

You see the gospel is everything.

If all I do is go round and care for people, even if I successfully help them with their issues, all I can be is a poor imitation of a social worker or counsellor. If I have nothing more than my take on things, my compassion and my practicality, ultimately I offer nothing that can transform their real future. But if I help them to get the gospel then everything changes. The gospel brings life.

I found it was similar with my beloved NHS. We can heal for a time, we can patch things up, we can extend life, but ultimately everyone dies. The NHS is never going to affect the mortality rate, which, when I last checked, was holding steady at one hundred percent!

So for those of you who haven't quite worked it out yet, here is a different way of telling the gospel. Unfortunately it's a true story.

I was sitting at home when the letter came through the door. It read something like this: 'Alan Snuggs, were you the driver of FL18 NFO on this date, and did you twice exceed the speed limit contrary to the Road Traffic Act?' I paused for thought. A number of excuses flooded my mind. I was having a bad day. I was unlucky. I didn't know it was there. I was lost. The truth is I had no excuse. The law is the law and I had broken it twice. With a heavy heart I filled in the form and accepted my guilt.

Not long after, another letter dropped though my door, hitting the mat like a heavy weight. It was my judgement. 'You have been found guilty, and you will pay a sixty pound fine, go on a driving awareness course (cost: ninety pounds) and have three points deducted from your licence. Also you need to contact your insurers so that they can increase your premium.'

Of course, I was not happy, but at least I bumped into some fellow church members at the driving awareness course!

All this got me thinking. What if God sent me a letter about all the times I have let him down?

What would that look like? Well, I knew it would be a long letter, a very long letter, and it would contain many things that would shame and embarrass me. Indeed, if my church members were to see it, they might not want me as a leader anymore. The more I thought about it, the more uncomfortable I became. In my imagination, it would have said something like this: 'Alan, did you really commit all these gross sins, was this really you?' And accompanying it would be one thick pile of papers, maybe enough to fill a room, maybe more. Every bad action, every wrong thought and judgement. And every lack: of integrity, of faith. Every horrible thought. Every ghastly sin.

Like with the speeding offence, perhaps my first thought would be to think of justifications. I had a bad day. It was their fault. I didn't mean to. I just forgot. I'm not really that bad, am I? But eventually, and very reluctantly, I would have to sign the form. 'Yes, it was me.'

And then suppose I had to wait for that second letter – you know, the one that confirms my penalty. Well, it's going to be death, isn't it? That is what the Bible says. But no letter arrives. I get anxious. I need to know. Where is my letter, what is my sentence? I ring heaven and ask. I just need to know. Tell me the worst. And then the guy at the other end says, 'Oh, we know all about you. Boy, do we know! We have your record here. But hang on, it says on your letter **DEBT PAID** in big red letters. You get to go free because of Jesus. He died on a cross, so God doesn't see your sin anymore. He only sees your righteousness.'

God sent Jesus for all of your sin. If you don't think you had a debt, think again. But he has paid it all. You are defined by what Jesus did, not by what you did. He has saved you.

This is amazing grace. Illogical, incredible, undeserved. But mine and yours nonetheless. Have you grasped this promise? It could be too good to be true, but maybe it is too good *not* to be true. It's a life changer, it really is, and it's all yours for the taking.

The door is wide open. Get the heck in!

Chapter Twenty
What's in a Miracle?

I gave in and admitted God was God.
CS Lewis

Simon was a committed atheist, but he hung around our social group in the early nineteen eighties. At the time we mainly met in the pubs of Victoria London. He seemed a nice guy, but he was quite shy and no one knew much about him, not even where he worked. Then one day God gave one of us a bit of insight into Simon (in churchy terms this is called a word of knowledge). The word was 'mushroom'. Now, I can tell you, the last thing in the world you want to do with a guy already a bit dubious about Christianity is go and tell him that God has a word for him and its mushroom! But we had faith, and tentatively, we shared it with Simon, ready to run away if he got annoyed! The thing is, he didn't get cross at all. In fact, he got all emotional. It turned out that he was a PHD student, and guess what he was studying? Mushrooms. Every day he stared at these intricate organisms, wondering if there really was a God. Well, now he knew God was on his case. He straight away gave his life to Jesus, and many years later he became a church leader. You see, to us miracles are, well, miracles. But to God they are everyday.

Yilmaz was a committed Muslim who lived in Turkey. In 2010 he was introduced to some friends of mine who were planting a Christian church in his country. Yilmaz listened to the gospel message and, after some thought and time, decided to become a Christian. For his wife, this was an outrage, and she refused to discuss anything to do with his new faith. She was furious. She thought only of the disgrace he had brought to the family. She was so furious she wanted to divorce him.

Then one night she had a dream. Someone who called himself Jesus appeared before her. This Jesus said to her, 'Why are you rejecting my church?' Then he showed her the red marks on his hand, where iron nails might have been driven. She was startled, and the next day decided to visit Yilmaz's church. But the sense of shame still got to her, and she soon left and went back home. That night she had the same dream. Again, Jesus said, 'Why are you rejecting my church?' Again he showed her his nail marks. This happened several nights in a row. Eventually she realised that what she was seeing was real, and after a few weeks of attending the church, she committed her life to the same Jesus that her husband was following. She and Yilmaz are now leaders in that same church.

It might seem odd to think God can appear in a vision in the modern day. This somehow seems different than visions in the distant past. But I have heard that kind of story so many times, and always from people I trust. Miracles happen. Maybe not as much as some would like, but they still happen. Sometimes we might pray for a miracle and receive no answer. My list of cancer patients over the years is testimony to that. But then again, this only reminds me of a woman in my church, who prayed for the healing of a growth in her womb. The NHS couldn't accept it when they found it had disappeared. They insisted on scan after scan until they finally had to admit defeat.

Every Easter we celebrate another miracle, one that happened two thousand years ago. One that changed the world for ever. Yet at least half the world will carry on ignoring the very fact of the resurrection. Most people in this country don't even know what Easter is for.

I have often mused on the evidence for the resurrection. To be blunt, if Jesus did not rise from the dead, then death beat him, and my hope for eternity is nothing but a sham. The apostle Paul, a one-time killer of Christians, who, like Yilmaz's wife famously met Jesus in a vision, said this: 'And if Christ has not been raised, our preaching is useless and so is your faith.' He then says that, if this is the case, then we are to be pitied more than all men. (Thankfully, he does go on to testify that indeed Christ has been raised from the dead!)

I am aware that many historians and lawyers have looked into this truth. Some, such as Frank Morrison, who wrote a book called *Who Moved the Stone?*, started their research as committed atheists, determined to prove that Jesus could not have risen from the dead. However, he, like so many others, became convinced that Jesus did rise from the dead.

I was schooled in the whole business of looking for evidence, firstly as a law student and then as a police officer. I still remember today cases that were won or lost on the quality of evidence that I produced. To me, the case for the resurrection is overwhelming. But I'll let the jury decide. Here is just some of the evidence:

If not the resurrection, what happened two thousand years ago that so changed the disciples? When Jesus was crucified, his band of brothers ran for their lives. They were timid and fearful. What transformed them into men willing to die for their faith? In this world, many individuals claim to be messiahs, but once they are exposed, their followers just fall away. That just didn't happen with Jesus. To me, the transformation of this little band of feeble men is totally compelling.

James, Jesus' half brother, was originally opposed to his brother's claims. In fact, during Jesus' early ministry, the Bible tells us that his family thought him deranged. A total transformation occurred in James after he saw his brother resurrected from the dead. How could Jesus have convinced his own brother, and indeed his own mother, if the resurrection had not taken place? Why would his own family start to worship him as God if they still thought it was one big con trick?

Jesus' resurrection was confirmed by even his most bitter enemies, such as Paul. Paul initially hated Christians so much that he killed them. What transformed him into the leader of the new church? Why would he change his very beliefs, the direction of his entire life, unless he knew the truth?

The early church stopped worshipping on Saturday, as Jews had done for thousands of years, and suddenly began worshipping on Sunday. The Sabbath was sacred to the Jews. What had happened to change all this, other than the fact that the resurrection occurred on a Sunday?

Not only was the day of worship changed, but so too was the object of worship. Considering that one of the Ten Commandments forbids the worship of false gods, it is impossible to conceive of devout Jews simply switching their worship to Jesus without proof of his divinity.

What else but a risen Christ could explain the rapid growth and extraordinary commitment of the early church?

Even non-Christian historians of the time, such as Josephus and Suetonius, record that Jesus appeared to his disciples on the third day.

If Jesus had not risen from the dead, all the Romans would have had to do to nip Christianity in the bud was produce the body. They couldn't! Because he was risen.

There are, of course, counter theories that have been put forward to explain the events of two thousand years ago. My favourite is the one that says that Jesus wasn't completely dead when he was taken down from the cross. Anyone who has the least amount of understanding of the act of crucifixion would laugh this one out of court. The Romans knew how to kill; no one survived crucifixion. In any case, at this point in the history of the Roman Empire, soldiers were instructed to ensure that their victims were dead before their removal from the cross. This is why a Roman soldier pierced Jesus' body with a spear – just to make sure.

The resurrection of Jesus was a stunning miracle. And it is one that millions believe. Everyone has a choice. You can stand with the cynics and discount any possibility of a miracle, or you can decide to thank God for the greatest miracle of all. I for one believe it.

Who knows what might happen tomorrow? I feel optimistic, even a little confident.

We could all do with a miracle or two.

Chapter Twenty-One
Stopping the Lonely Rooms

*You have not lived today until you have done something
for someone who can never repay you.*
John Bunyan

My friend Bobbie has cerebral palsy and is partially
sighted. His best friend is his dog, Herbie. Though
to be frank, Herbie is not the best guide dog in the world;
he has been known to steal food from Morrisons, and
sometimes even from children! But Herbie is Bobbie's
best friend. Recently Bobbie wrote a moving poem about
Herbie. In it, he talks about Herbie as being the one that
'stops the lonely rooms'. I just love that phrase.

If the church did what it is supposed to do, how many
lonely rooms could it stop?

Wally and Karen Gowing are fervent Liverpool
supporters. Each year they kindly arrange for me to come
and see Liverpool play my beloved West Ham at Anfield.
We always lose badly, and that is probably why the
Liverpool fans are so pleased to see me! I have, however,
noticed something special about Wally and Karen over
the years. They exude love and pastoral care to those
Liverpool fans around them, especially those in need.

Nothing is ever too much trouble. Wherever they are, they gather their football family around them, making sure everyone is OK. It's actually quite mind-blowing to watch.

Charlie Keenan was one of the world's greatest surgeons. It was said that if Charlie couldn't help you, then nobody could. He was the most brilliant, dynamic consultant I had the privilege to meet in my whole NHS career. But he was also an enigmatic character – someone who could make the life of any hospital director a complete nightmare.

We were introduced in 1990, in Birmingham. Charlie, a renowned figure in the world of oncology, and me, an aspiring young hospital director hoping to make his mark. Charlie introduced himself in his own inimitable fashion: throwing his briefcase across the room at me, shouting, 'The last guy who occupied your position didn't last very long, and nor will you!' I was startled, to the say the least, but I had been forewarned that this was Charlie's way. I tried not to let it get to me too much. But boy was he a demanding, aggressive, precocious *pain in the backside*. He gave me a torrid time in my first few months. Nothing ever seemed good enough. But gradually his attitude changed, and suddenly, as if by magic, we were good friends.

Charlie was made a clinical director with some management responsibility, and myself and a senior nurse were tasked with helping him. I began to enjoy our meetings and would often gown up and meet him in theatre, where he would explain to me some of his pioneering approaches. At that time, the government had introduced the 'internal market' into the NHS, and

Charlie and I began to think of ways we could increase the revenue coming into the hospital. Sometimes we even used to go around Birmingham late at night, talking to GPs and getting them to refer more of their work our way. It was exciting, ground-breaking. The hospital's revenue increased markedly.

One Christmas I was invited to Charlie's annual Christmas dinner. He put this on for all his staff, including nurses and fellow doctors. It was a sumptuous affair held in Birmingham's top Chinese restaurant. As I got up to leave, a member of his nursing staff informed me that I must be truly blessed, as generally Charlie didn't like managers. He had never invited somebody like me to one of his dinners before. I did feel a little proud.

But here is the thing I most remember about Charlie: he wasn't a saint. He had a reputation as a hard man, someone with a difficult past; someone who had fought his way up to become the very best. A man you tangled with at your peril. And also, by now, a very rich man, with a huge private practice. But one night I got to see the true Charlie, the man behind the facade.

I visited the hospital late at night, for what reason I can't remember. As I walked through the hospital, I met the senior nurse manager. 'Come and look at this,' she said. She led me to the gynaecological ward, where a group of patients were sitting around a woman. The woman was sitting up in bed, drinking a pint of beer. Next to her was a smiling and energised Charlie, holding court and making everyone laugh. 'Before you ask,' said the senior nurse manager, 'the lady you can see is dying, she has only a few days to live. She wanted to have a pint of beer, so Charlie arranged for us all to have a pub night around her bed. That's the kind of man he is. But please don't ever tell anyone – he wouldn't be too happy.'

I watched the happy crowd for a few minutes. Charlie saw me and waved. Something got me right inside, and I think I shed a tear. Humanity can sometimes be selfish, miserable and grasping, but sometimes it can be magnificent as well.

It's in us all. Our father put it there.

We can all stop some lonely rooms.

Chapter Twenty-Two
The Lost Sheep

Well I came home
Like a stone
And I fell heavy into your arms.
These days of dust
Which we've known
Will blow away with this new sun.
Mumford and Sons, 'I Will Wait'

Jesus once told a story about a shepherd who had a hundred sheep. One day, when one went missing, the shepherd left the other ninety nine to go looking for it. Difficult to believe? Well, it happens today.

Several years ago, when my marriage was struggling and life seemed hard, my faith began to drift. I found the church Nicole and I were in at the time completely unhelpful, almost a burden rather than a help. I began to have doubts, and though I never lost my faith, I think it would be true to say that I wandered away from God, that I lost that personal relationship with him that thankfully I have back now.

Jesus had another story: of the prodigal son, a young guy who turns his back on his father and squanders his wealth in wild living. When things turn sour and the money runs out, he seeks his father, willing to become one of his hired hands in order to get back on his feet. He is little prepared for the reaction he gets. The father, seeing him in the distance, is filled with compassion and, running to his son, throws his arms around him. He then puts on the biggest celebratory feast, where he announces to everyone, 'This son of mine was dead and is alive again; he was lost and is found.'

What happened to me was perhaps less dramatic, but the story of the prodigal son resonates deeply.

As I was saying, I was fed up with church. But still I managed to find myself at a Christian festival called Spring Harvest with Nicole and our young children. I was determined to avoid anything too spiritual. I figured that I would be safe with a concert. There was a singer on called Martin Joseph, who had the reputation for being edgy and a little cynical, and I thought that this would suit me just fine. The night of the performance I sat in the furthest, darkest seat at the back of the auditorium. It was all going well, but then he sang a song that ripped me apart. It was called 'What If God was One of Us' and it just broke me. I knew God was speaking to me, that I was lost, but that my father was letting me know that he forgave me my wandering. So began a long walk back, for which I am eternally grateful.

Some months later I was on a family holiday in Croyde, North Devon. Late at night I decided to go body surfing. It was a glorious evening, and I was quite alone as I enthusiastically threw myself into wave after wave. I was filled with inexpressible joy, the sort that young kids get when Christmas day comes. Now call me mad if you want, but I am sure I heard God laughing. It was quite remarkable. You see, God loves it when the prodigals return.

Philip Yancey retells Jesus' story of the prodigal son through a remarkable true tale about a prodigal daughter, a seventeen-year-old girl who runs off to Detroit and spends a year as a prostitute. At first, she believes this to be the time of her life. But just as in the story of the prodigal son, after a short time it all goes horribly wrong. She becomes ill as the drugs take their effect; the 'boss man' kicks her out; she ends up living on the streets in downtown Detroit. She thinks, 'God, why did I leave? My dog back home eats better than I do.' She knows in a flash she needs to go home. She leaves an answer phone message on her parents' home phone. 'Dad, Mom, it's me. I was wondering about maybe coming home. I am catching a bus up your way. If you are not at the bus station when it gets in at midnight, I will go on until it hits Canada.' Her bus journey takes seven hours. Seven hours to think about what she will say to her dad. By the time the bus finally gets into her home town, she is nervous and afraid. Will anyone be there? Do they even want her back, after all she has done?

Let me share the conclusion just as Philip Yancey tells it:

> ...not one of the thousand scenes that have played out in her mind prepares her for what she sees. There in the bus terminal in Traverse City Michigan stands a group of forty brothers, and sisters and great aunts and uncles and cousins and a grandmother and

great grandmother to boot. They are wearing goofy party hats and blowing noise makers and taped across the entire wall of the terminal is a computer generated banner that reads 'welcome home'. Out of the crowd of well wishers breaks her dad. She stares out through tears quivering in her eyes like hot mercury and begins the memorised speech, 'Dad I'm sorry, I know...' He interrupts her. 'Hush, child, we've got no time for that, no time for apologies. You'll be late for the party. A banquet is waiting for you at home.

I once knew a seventeen year old who left home and became a prostitute, just like the girl in the story. Her name was Cheryl and she was beautiful. I have good reason to remember her: one night, whilst arresting her for assault, she stuck her nail deep into my hand, leaving a small permanent scar. I often wonder what happened to her, but sadly have little doubt about her fate.

God never gives up on us. He waits patiently, lovingly, waiting for us to come to him. The gospel of grace begins and ends with forgiveness. Grace alone melts our hardness and mess. As Philip Yancey says:

'We are accustomed to finding a catch in every promise, but Jesus' stories of extravagant grace include no catch, no loophole disqualifying us from God's love. Each has at its core an ending too good to be true – or so good that it must be true.'

It's a grace that has saved me, as well as billions of other Christians. I for one am grateful to my core.

Are you missing the party?

Chapter Twenty Three
Big Trees

*When the church is functioning as it's supposed to do,
in all its messiness, it's a wonderful thing, a
supernatural thing that no amount of mere
neighbourliness can match.*
Steve Furtick

I don't know whether you have ever returned to a place
long ago significant in your life. I guess it's always a
bit of a risk. Nicole and I never go on holiday to the same
place twice, no matter how marvellous the original
experience. We just know it will never be the same. But
sometimes I just can't help myself. Once it was a church
that, when I had known it, had been so vibrant and full
of life; when we visited it just felt dead. On another
occasion, I revisited my old university halls of residence,
only to find that they had been knocked down. The halls
had apparently been full of asbestos! And then there was
our one-time favourite pub, The Red Cow, on our return
nothing more than a square of concrete.

But there was one place that was special: Saint
Michael's church in Chester Square, London, which we
returned to for the first time in over thirty five years one

autumn day. For us, this had been a significant place. Nicole and I had met here, become Christians here, had married here. Would our return be anti-climactic? Would we be welcomed? Surely no one would still know us.

It turned out that Saint Michael's was hosting a women's Christian conference, so I immediately felt a little out of place! But we were greeted by two very cheerful women, who asked us why we were visiting. We told them how we had been part of a very small group of young Christians who had wanted to be more expressive in our worship. The church had allowed us to hold an evening service to explore such possibilities. It had transformed our lives, but as we numbered just twenty-five people, we had had to battle to keep the service going.

What followed moved us to tears. Both women thanked us for fighting for that service, so many years ago. Then they told us what the church was doing in the modern day. Apparently that night they were hosting an alternative Halloween service for the local community. Over one thousand families were coming. Yes, you read that right, over one thousand!

On our way out, I asked these two lovely women a question that had been on my mind throughout our conversation. You see, those many years ago, we had met for our evening service in a small side chapel. But looking round, I just couldn't figure out where the side chapel had gone. The two women laughed. 'The thing is, because of the growth of the church, we have an alternative use for it.' They then led us through a door and showed us a small room which was now a cloakroom. Once upon a time, it had been our meeting place! But now, given their growth, it was a place where people hung their coats.

As we wandered through Pimlico neither Nicole or I spoke. We just smiled. We may believe we are so important to God's plan, and perhaps sometimes we are, but the fact is that he is always achieving amazing stuff anyway. In those thirty-five years, the church had grown and grown. Out of a tiny group of people, it had evolved and matured into something that touched every part of its community.

Paul writes this to the Ephesians:

'Now to him who is able to do immeasurably more than all we ask or imagine, according to his power that is at work within us, to him be glory in the church and in Christ Jesus throughout all generations forever and ever!'

Sometimes we struggle and strain in laying down our few seeds, wondering the whole time whether any of it is worthwhile. But out of small seeds, God grows big trees.

Chapter Twenty-Four
Best Seats in the House

Just come to the table.
Come join the sinners. You have been redeemed.
Take your place beside the Saviour now.
Sit down and be set free.
Come to the table.
Just come to the table.

The Sidewalk Prophets, 'Come to the Table'

It had been a fairly boring shift for PC Alan Snuggs of the Metropolitan Police's Incident Support Unit.

It was 1983 and I was in central London, standing outside a well known theatre, waiting for an Irish Protestant protest march to go by. We had been expecting trouble, but none had arrived. The march was quietly petering out, and it would soon be time to get back into our carrier. My colleagues were amusing themselves, talking to the girls at the box office, trying to negotiate free tickets and maybe a date or two. I was bored and a little fed up; it would still be hours before I got home to our flat in Regency Street. It was only a couple of miles away, but I would have to go back to Chiswick with my unit, and then travel all the way back into central London all over again. I noticed the theatre was presenting a musical with Griff Rhys Jones in the lead role. It was their opening night. I would have given anything to be there.

A rather scruffy man wearing jeans and a t-shirt wandered out of the theatre with a mug of coffee in his hand. We started talking. 'I can see that your colleagues are trying to get a few freebies,' he observed.

'Yes, that would be typical,' I said, thinking of the many times I had stood by embarrassed as they used their police uniforms to get anything from free burgers to access to clubs and cinemas.

'Do you like the theatre?' the man asked. Well, as it happened, Nicole and I loved nothing more than to visit the West End to experience the vibrancy of the theatre, not that we could afford to do this often. At my answer, the man seemed to spring to life, talking about all the shows he had seen and been involved with. I assumed he was just another member of the box office staff.

My inspector waved frantically at me from across the road, and I reluctantly informed the man I needed to be on my way. I had really enjoyed our conversation. 'Just hang on,' he said. 'I have something for you.' He ran into the theatre and came back with two tickets. 'You have no idea who I am, do you? I confirmed in the affirmative, hoping I didn't offend. 'Well, that doesn't matter,' he said breezily. 'But what does matter is that I am the king of theatre round here, and I want you and your wife to come to our opening night tonight. Here, these are the best tickets in the house. When you come, please do say hello. I may be dressed slightly differently, and there will be TV cameras around, but please introduce me to your wife. I would love to meet her.'

I was made up, if not a little bemused. And of course we took him up on his offer. We had a fabulous evening. Our seats were like thrones, centre front row, padded and raised. But we were far too shy to say hello to the guy, who, as he had warned me he would be, was dressed up to the nines in a velvet suit. He was surrounded by the media. I was told it was Sir Andrew Lloyd Webber, but I can't be totally sure. Whatever, the tickets were a kind and generous gesture to a stranger, and I appreciated it.

As I drove back to Chiswick with my by now extremely jealous colleagues, I reflected on something that I have thought a lot about in the years since that wonderful day. Who is it that is really worth meeting? Who is it that is really worth knowing?

Through the grace of God, I have been able to do a few interesting things in my life. I have felt the thrill of a one-hundred-and-twenty-mile-an-hour police chase, a helicopter flying just a few feet above. I have supped tea with prime ministers, as well as miners. I have watched the sun set in Auckland Harbour and rise on the plains of Africa. I have swum in the turquoise waters of the Mediterranean and enjoyed the surf of the Australian Gold Coast. I have eaten at the best curry house in Hyderabad and in the poorest shack in Maseru. I have helped build hospitals, new organisations, churches, even a crazy cafe. I have a wonderful wife, two remarkable children and more friends than I could possibly deserve. But I have also screwed up and got things wrong. I have been on the brink, and in the darkest places.

But through it all I have had someone by my side.

Someone I know. Someone called Jesus. For me nothing can compare to knowing Jesus. Nothing comes remotely close. The biggest thing in my life is knowing him.

You may look for other things: relationships, money, a good career, power, pleasure... But one day it will all be gone. Jesus was not 'nice'. He didn't sit around singing hymns and smiling at everyone. He was radical. He walked on water, overturned tables, healed lepers, drank with outcasts, and turned water into wine. He mocked the religious leaders of the day and got right into their faces. He brought forgiveness and truth. He died for our sins. He embodied pure love. He is the king. He always was.

And he has the best tickets in the house waiting just for you – because he is that kind of king, that kind of father, that kind of friend. One great saviour, one great father. The real deal. There is no one else like him.

I am surrounded by Jesus and so are you.

Do you know him?

About the Author

Alan Snuggs was brought up in Bournemouth, Dorset. He gained a law degree at Exeter University and in 1981 joined the police graduate scheme in London. Five years later he joined the NHS graduate scheme, becoming a hospital director and then a trust chief executive in the West Midlands. He subsequently formed a business focussing on governance and innovation and worked closely with the Department of Health.

Alan also helped start up a vibrant church coffee shop in Buxton, Derbyshire, the proceeds of which supported a poor community in South Africa. From his early twenties, Alan has been involved in church leadership, most recently supporting and developing young leaders, as well as encouraging guys that Jesus is relevant to them.

He is married to Nicole, and they have two grown up children, James and Jessica. He currently lives in North Wales and is part of North Coast Church as well as supporting the new Lighthouse Church on Anglesey.